ESSENTIALS OF ANALYST ENGAGEMENT

Mastering Analyst Relations for Influencing the Influencers

SAURABH BISHT

ISBN 979-8-89186-594-5

CONTENTS

WHY I WROTE THIS BOOK

Welcome to *"Essentials of Analyst Engagement: Mastering Analyst Relations for influencing the influencers."* In today's competitive landscape, establishing strong connections and strategic partnerships is crucial for achieving remarkable business success. Throughout my years of experience and observation, I have witnessed the transformative impact that strategic relationships with industry analysts can have on a company's growth and influence.

I wrote this book with a clear purpose—to provide entrepreneurs, marketing professionals, and business leaders like you with the knowledge, insights, and strategies to leverage the power of analyst relationships. "Essentials of Analyst Engagement" serves as your comprehensive guide, offering practical advice and actionable techniques to navigate the complexities of analyst relations and unlock hidden opportunities.

Discover how to build, nurture, and harness the power of analyst relations to unlock hidden opportunities, amplify brand influence, and skyrocket revenue. From understanding the analyst landscape to crafting impactful communications, measuring results, and staying ahead of trends, this book empowers you to transform your business and achieve unparalleled success.

Through the pages of "Essentials of Analyst Engagement," I invite you on a transformative journey—a journey to unlock the power of strategic relationships and elevate your business to new heights. Together, let's build bridges that connect you with influential analysts, unlock extraordinary achievements, and create a lasting impact in your industry.

Get ready to unleash the power of strategic relationships and embark on a path toward unparalleled business success. Let's begin this journey together and build bridges that will shape the future of your business.

CHAPTER 1

INTRODUCTION TO ANALYST RELATIONS AND ITS IMPORTANCE

1.1 Understanding Why Analyst Relations Matters

In today's tech-driven world, the role of analysts has become increasingly important in shaping the opinions of key stakeholders such as customers, investors, and the media. They provide in-depth insights, analysis, and recommendations on a company's products, services, and market position. Therefore, it is essential for organizations to effectively engage with analysts and ensure they have a favourable view of the company.

Analyst relations involve a set of activities aimed at building and maintaining a relationship with industry analysts. This relationship is crucial in terms of building a company's reputation, improving product visibility, and increasing sales. Analysts have a significant influence on the industry, and their opinions and recommendations can make or break a company's success. The primary goal of AR is to build and maintain positive relationships with industry analysts, influencers, and thought leaders who influence the perceptions and purchasing decisions of a company's target audience.

Analyst relations (AR) is a crucial component of any organization's public relations and communications strategy. The benefits of a strong AR program are numerous and can impact a company's bottom line in numerous ways.

For example, a positive relationship with analysts can lead to increased media coverage and visibility, improved market reputation and brand recognition, and increased sales and revenue.

Despite its importance, AR is often neglected or given low priority within organizations. And most of the well know products and services companies only want to be in the branded reports published by these companies or in a review video. However, companies that prioritize AR and invest in improving the overall business process and product benefits can see the value it brings to their overall communication and marketing efforts.

Investing in analyst relations can be beneficial for companies in several ways:

- ✔ **Thought leadership:** Engaging with analysts and participating in analyst events can help a company establish itself as a thought leader in its industry and showcase its expertise to a wider audience, which can help drive new business and revenue opportunities.

- ✔ **Market insight:** By participating in analyst reports, companies can gain a deeper understanding of their industry and the market trends that are affecting it, allowing them to make informed business decisions.

- ✔ **Reputation management:** Analyst reports can impact a company's reputation in the market, so engaging with analysts and participating in these reports can help a company ensure that its reputation is accurately represented.

- ✔ **Customer validation:** Analyst reports can also be used to validate a company's products, services, and business strategies to customers, partners, and investors.

- ✔ **Improved decision making:** By engaging with analysts, companies can gain access to research, insights, and market intelligence that can help inform their decision making and business strategy.

- ✔ **Networking opportunities:** Participating in analyst events provides opportunities to network with other industry players and thought leaders, which can help a company build relationships and identify new business opportunities, leading to increased revenue.

While being featured in analyst reports or review videos can provide valuable exposure, the true value of AR lies in the insights, recommendations, and market intelligence that analysts can provide. By actively engaging with analysts and seeking their expertise, companies gain access to in-depth knowledge about market trends, competitive landscapes, and customer preferences. This information can inform product development, marketing strategies, and overall business decision-making.

Overall, investing in analyst relations can help companies stay informed, stay ahead of industry trends, and establish themselves as leaders in their respective markets.

Investing in AR also demonstrates a company's commitment to transparency, industry collaboration, and thought leadership. By fostering relationships with analysts, organizations show their willingness to engage in meaningful discussions, share insights, and contribute to the industry's overall growth and development. This proactive approach can help position companies as trusted partners and industry leaders.

Here are a few general examples of companies that have publicly discussed the benefits of engaging with analysts:

- **IBM:** IBM has a strong commitment to analyst relations and has been recognized as a Leader by Gartner in multiple Magic Quadrants. The company has emphasized the importance of engaging with analysts to stay ahead of industry trends and drive business growth. In a recent statement, an IBM spokesperson highlighted the benefits of engaging with analysts, saying, "By working with analyst firms, we are able to stay informed on the latest market trends, validate our products and services, and showcase our expertise to a wider audience."

- **Microsoft:** Microsoft is another company that has invested heavily in analyst relations and has been recognized as a Leader by Gartner in multiple Magic Quadrants. The company has credited its engagement with analysts for helping it stay ahead of industry trends and drive revenue growth. In a recent interview, a Microsoft spokesperson stated, "Our investment in analyst relations has been critical in helping us stay informed on market trends and validate our products and services. Engaging with analysts has allowed us to build strong relationships and establish ourselves as thought leaders in our industry."

- **SAP:** SAP is well-known for its commitment to analyst relations and has consistently been recognized as a Leader by Gartner in various Magic Quadrants. The company has credited its strong relationship with analysts as a key factor in driving its business success and staying ahead of the competition. In a recent statement, an SAP executive emphasized the importance of working with analyst firms, saying, "By engaging with analysts, we are able to gain valuable insights into the market, validate our solutions, and showcase our expertise. Our investment in analyst relations has been a key driver in our success and has helped us stay ahead of the competition."

These examples demonstrate the benefits that companies such as IBM, Microsoft, and SAP have seen from investing in analyst relations. By engaging with analysts, they have been able to gain valuable insights into the market, validate their solutions, and establish themselves as thought leaders in their respective industries. This has helped these companies stay ahead of industry trends and drive growth.

1.2 The Importance of Building Strong Relationships with Analysts

Building strong relationships with analysts is crucial for technology companies. Analysts are influential individuals who have the power to shape market perceptions of a company's products and services. As such, it is important for product marketing, analyst relations managers, PR managers, and influencer relationship managers to prioritize building relationships with analysts.

One of the key benefits of building strong relationships with analysts is the ability to gain valuable insights into the market. Analysts have a deep understanding of the industry and can provide companies with valuable information about market trends, customer preferences, and competitors. By developing strong relationships with analysts, companies can gain access to these insights, which can help them make better-informed business decisions.

In addition to gaining insights, building strong relationships with analysts can also help companies to increase their visibility in the market. Analysts are often quoted in media publications and are frequently called upon to provide insights and commentary on industry developments. By building relationships with analysts, companies can increase their visibility in the market and position themselves as thought leaders in their industry.

Another benefit of building strong relationships with analysts is the ability to improve product development. Analysts can provide feedback on products and services, which can help companies to refine their offerings and better meet customer needs. By developing strong relationships with analysts, companies can gain access to this feedback and use it to improve their products and services.

Finally, building strong relationships with analysts can help companies to build trust with customers and partners. Analysts have a reputation for being objective and unbiased, which means that their endorsements can carry a lot of weight. By developing strong relationships with analysts, companies can gain their endorsement and build trust with customers and partners.

In conclusion, building strong relationships with analysts is essential for technology companies. It can help them gain valuable insights, increase their visibility in the market, improve product development, and build trust with customers and partners. As such, product marketing, analyst relations managers, PR managers, and influencer relationship managers should prioritize building relationships with analysts as part of their overall strategy for managing analyst relations.

In this book, we will explore the fundamentals of AR and provide strategies and best practices for building and maintaining successful relationships with analysts. We will also delve into the challenges and opportunities in the analyst relations landscape and provide practical tips for measuring the impact of AR efforts. Whether you are a seasoned AR professional or just starting out, this book will provide you with the tools and knowledge you need to effectively engage with analysts and achieve your organizational goals.

Notes

CHAPTER **2**

UNDERSTANDING THE ANALYST LANDSCAPE AND INFLUENCER ECOSYSTEM

The analyst landscape is a complex and constantly evolving environment, and it is essential for organizations to understand it to effectively engage with analysts. In this chapter, we will explore the different types of analysts and their areas of expertise, as well as the role they play in shaping industry opinions and purchasing decisions.

2.1　The Role of Analysts in Tech Industry

Analysts are a crucial component of the technology industry and play a critical role in shaping the perception and success of tech companies. They are experts in their field, with deep knowledge and insights into emerging trends, market dynamics, and consumer behaviour. Their analysis and recommendations are highly respected and valued by industry stakeholders, including investors, media, and business leaders.

In the tech industry, analysts are primarily responsible for providing research, insights, and recommendations to assist companies in making informed decisions about their products, services, and strategies. They offer a unique perspective on the industry, providing an unbiased and objective analysis of market trends, competitive landscape, and customer needs. Analysts help tech companies to identify new opportunities, mitigate risks, and stay ahead of the competition.

- ✔ **Product Marketing:** Product marketing teams can leverage the insights provided by analysts to develop effective marketing strategies. Analysts can help product marketers to understand the competitive landscape, identify market gaps, and develop messaging that resonates with customers. By collaborating with analysts, product marketing teams can ensure that their products are positioned to meet customer needs and expectations.

- ✔ **Analyst Relations Manager:** Analyst relations managers are responsible for building and maintaining relationships with analysts. They understand the importance of analysts in shaping the perception of their company and work to ensure that analysts have access to the information they need to provide accurate and informed analysis. Analyst relations managers also work to ensure that their company is represented in the best possible light in analyst reports and recommendations.

- ✔ **PR Manager:** PR managers work to ensure that their company is well-positioned in the media. They understand that analysts are a critical component of media coverage and work to build relationships with analysts to ensure that their company is represented positively in analyst reports. PR managers can also use the insights provided by analysts to develop effective media strategies and messaging.

- ✔ **Influencer Relationship Manager:** Influencer relationship managers work to identify and build relationships with key influencers in the industry. Analysts are critical influencers, and relationship managers should work to ensure that analysts have access to the information they need to provide accurate and informed analysis. By building relationships with analysts, influencer relationship managers can ensure that their company is positioned positively in the industry.

In conclusion, analysts play a critical role in the tech industry by providing insights, research, and recommendations to help companies make informed decisions. Product marketing, analyst relations managers, PR managers, and influencer relationship managers all have a role to play in building strong relationships with analysts and leveraging their insights to drive success for their companies.

2.1.1 Different Types of Analysts

- **Industry Analysts**: They provide insights and analysis on a specific market or industry, such as technology or financial services. For example, Toni Sacconaghi from Sanford C. Bernstein & Co. LLC is a well-known industry analyst who provides insights and analysis on the technology sector, specifically on hardware and software companies.

- **Vertical Analysts**: They focus on specific vertical markets, such as healthcare or retail, and provide in-depth analysis on the trends and challenges in these markets. For instance, Dr. Vishal S. Mehta from Jefferies is a vertical analyst who focuses on the healthcare sector and provides in-depth analysis on trends and challenges in the industry.

- **Horizontal Analysts:** They cover cross-industry topics, such as cloud computing or artificial intelligence, and provide a broader view of these technologies across different industries. For example, Mark Murphy from JP Morgan Chase is a horizontal analyst who covers topics such as cloud computing and artificial intelligence across different industries.

- **Influencer Analysts:** They have a strong online presence and engage with a large audience through social media and blogs. They have a significant impact on industry opinion and purchasing decisions. For instance, Ben Thompson from Stratechery is an influencer analyst who has a strong online presence and engages with a large audience through his blog and social media. He has significant influence on industry opinions and purchasing decisions.

It is essential for organizations to understand the different types of analysts and their areas of expertise to effectively engage with them. This can be accomplished by regularly monitoring analyst reports and tracking the analysts' areas of focus and opinions on the company and its competitors.

In addition to industry analysts, it is important to understand the influencer ecosystem and the role that influencer analysts play in shaping industry opinions and purchasing decisions. These influencer analysts often have large online followings and significant influence over the opinions of potential customers and investors.

Some of the largest and most well-known analyst firms include Gartner, Forrester, and IDC. These firms provide extensive research and analysis on a wide range of industries and technologies. Gartner is well known for its Magic Quadrant (MQ), which provides a graphical representation of a market's direction, maturity, and participants, and helps organizations understand the market and their position within it. Forrester, on the other hand, is known for its Wave, which evaluates and ranks technology providers based on their current offering, strategy, and market presence. IDC provides market intelligence and insights, and is known for its MarketScape, which provides an in-depth analysis of a market and its participants.

Here are the details just in case any software industry reader wants to read further.

- **Gartner:** Gartner is a research and advisory company that provides technology-related insights for IT and other business leaders. It was founded in 1979 and is headquartered in Stamford, Connecticut, USA. The CEO of Gartner as of my knowledge cutoff is Manuel Camargo. Gartner provides a variety of reports and research services, including Magic Quadrant reports, Market Share reports, and Vendor Ratings reports, among others. These reports cover a range of technology-related topics, including cloud computing, artificial intelligence, cybersecurity, and digital transformation, among others.

- **Forrester Research:** Forrester is a leading research and advisory firm that provides market research and insights to help companies understand customers, markets, and technology trends. Forrester is headquartered in Cambridge, Massachusetts, USA. The CEO of Forrester is George F.

Colony. The market cap of Forrester as of 2022 is approximately $540 million USD. Some of the notable research reports published by Forrester include "Forrester Wave" which evaluates various technology vendors based on their products, services and strategies in different markets and "Forrester Marketspace" which provides insights into market trends and their impact on different industries.

- **IDC:** IDC is a leading market intelligence and research firm that provides data, insights, and analysis on technology and telecom markets worldwide. IDC is headquartered in Framingham, Massachusetts, USA. The CEO of IDC is Crawford Del Prete. The revenue of IDC is not publicly disclosed. IDC's research reports include "IDC MarketScape" which provides analysis and evaluation of technology vendors and "IDC FutureScape" which provides insights into future technology trends.

- **ISG:** Information Services Group (ISG) is a research and advisory firm that provides market intelligence and analysis on the technology industry, including areas such as digital transformation and cloud computing. ISG's research reports include "ISG Provider Lens" which evaluates service providers in various technology markets and "ISG Index" which provides insights into the state of the technology industry.

- **HFS Research:** HFS Research is a technology research and advisory firm that provides research and analysis on the technology market, including areas such as digital transformation and cloud computing. HFS is headquartered in Princeton, New Jersey, USA. The CEO of HFS is Phil Fersht. The revenue of HFS is not publicly disclosed. HFS's research reports include "HFS Blueprint Reports" which provide analysis and evaluation of technology service providers and "HFS Hot Vendors" which provides insights into emerging technology vendors.

- **Frost & Sullivan:** Frost & Sullivan is a growth strategy consulting firm that provides market research and analysis on a range of industries, including technology, healthcare, and energy. The CEO of Frost & Sullivan is Akash Saraf. The revenue of Frost & Sullivan is not publicly disclosed. Frost & Sullivan's research reports include "Frost & Sullivan Market Engineering" which provides market sizing, forecasting and segmentation analysis, and "Frost & Sullivan Industry Quotient" which provides insights into the growth opportunities of different industries.

- **MarketsandMarkets:** MarketsandMarkets is a market research firm that provides research and analysis on a range of industries, including technology, healthcare, and energy. MarketsandMarkets's research reports include "MarketsandMarkets Market Research Reports" which provide market size, share and forecast analysis and "MarketsandMarkets Industry Analysis" which provides insights into the growth opportunities of different industries.

- **Ovum:** Ovum is a market intelligence and research firm that provides research and analysis on a range of industries, including technology, telecommunications, and media. The CEO of Ovum is Ian Brow. Ovum's research reports include "Ovum Decision Matrix" which provides analysis and evaluation of technology vendors and "Ovum Industry Trends" which provides insights into technology trends and their impact on different industries.

- **ARC Advisory Group:** ARC Advisory Group is a market research and consulting firm that provides research and analysis on a range of industries, including industrial automation, energy, and transportation. ARC Advisory Group is headquartered in Dedham, Massachusetts, USA. The CEO of ARC Advisory Group is David Simchi-Levi. ARC Advisory Group's research reports include "ARC View" which provides market analysis and forecasting and "ARC Evaluate" which provides analysis and evaluation of technology vendors.

- **VentureBeat Insights:** VentureBeat Insights is headquartered in San Francisco, California, USA. The CEO of VentureBeat Insights is Matt Marshall. VentureBeat Insights is a market research and intelligence firm that provides research and analysis on the technology industry, including areas such as artificial intelligence and virtual reality. VentureBeat Insights' research reports include "VentureBeat Insights Market Intelligence Reports" which provide market size, share and forecast analysis and

"VentureBeat Insights Industry Trends" which provides insights into the growth opportunities of different industries.

- **ABI Research:** ABI Research is a market intelligence and advisory firm that provides insights and recommendations on the technology and innovation landscape. ABI Research is headquartered in Oyster Bay, New York, USA. The CEO of ABI Research is Stuart Carlaw.

Companies participate in Magic Quadrant (MQ), Wave, and MarketScape type of reports, also known as branded research reports for several reasons:

- **Industry recognition:** Being included in an MQ, Wave, or MarketScape report can be a significant recognition for a company and can help position it as a leader in its industry.

- **Market intelligence:** These reports provide in-depth analysis and market intelligence on the technology landscape and help companies understand the competitive landscape and market trends.

- **Customer insights:** These reports can help companies understand the needs and preferences of their target customers, which can inform product development and marketing strategies.

- **Business planning:** The insights and market intelligence provided in these reports can help companies make informed business decisions and plan for future growth and success.

- **Benchmarking:** Companies can use the information in these reports to benchmark their performance against competitors and understand areas where they can improve.

Overall, participating in MQ, Wave, and MarketScape reports can provide valuable insights and recognition for companies and help them achieve their business goals.

By understanding the analyst landscape and influencer ecosystem, organizations can effectively target their AR efforts and build stronger relationships with the most relevant and influential analysts. This will help to increase their visibility and credibility in the industry and improve their overall market reputation.

Many companies go beyond participation in report and also showcase their product or solutions capabilities in the event hosted by these research firms. Some of the events are mentioned below

- **Gartner Symposium/ITxpo**: This is Gartner's largest and most comprehensive conference, offering a range of sessions and workshops, including keynotes, peer-to-peer discussions, and expert-led sessions.

- **Forrester Research Forum:** This is Forrester's flagship event, bringing together business and technology leaders to discuss the latest trends and challenges in technology, marketing, and customer experience.

- **IDC Directions:** This is IDC's premier conference, featuring keynotes and panel discussions from industry experts, as well as workshops and networking opportunities.

- **Gartner CIO Leadership Forum:** This is a specific event for CIOs, offering a range of sessions and workshops, including peer-to-peer discussions and expert-led sessions.

- **Forrester Wave Evaluation Methodology Workshop**: This workshop provides in-depth training on Forrester's Wave Evaluation Methodology, which is used to evaluate and rank technology solutions.

- **IDC Innovators:** This is a series of events hosted by IDC, highlighting innovation and emerging technology solutions in specific industries, such as healthcare and finance.

- **Gartner Data & Analytics Summit:** This summit is focused on data and analytics, offering a range of sessions and workshops, including keynotes, peer-to-peer discussions, and expert-led sessions.

- **Forrester Customer Experience Forum:** This forum is focused on customer experience, offering a range of sessions and workshops, including keynotes, peer-to-peer discussions, and expert-led sessions.

- **IDC FutureScape:** This is a series of events hosted by IDC, exploring the future of technology and its impact on various industries, such as healthcare and finance.

- **Gartner Supply Chain Executive Conference:** This conference is focused on supply chain management, offering a range of sessions and workshops, including keynotes, peer-to-peer discussions, and expert-led sessions.

- **Ovum Digital Transformation Summit:** Ovum hosts this event to discuss the latest trends and challenges in digital transformation and how they impact various industries.

- **Frost & Sullivan Executive MindXchange:** This is Frost & Sullivan's flagship event, offering a range of sessions and workshops, including keynotes, peer-to-peer discussions, and expert-led sessions.

- **ARC Advisory Group Industry Forum:** This is a series of events hosted by ARC Advisory Group, exploring the latest trends and challenges in various industries, such as manufacturing and energy.

- **HFS Blueprint Report Launch Event:** HFS launches its Blueprint Reports at this event, offering a range of sessions and workshops, including keynotes, peer-to-peer discussions, and expert-led sessions.

- **ABI Research Summit:** This summit is hosted by ABI Research, offering a range of sessions and workshops, including keynotes, peer-to-peer discussions, and expert-led sessions.

- **VentureBeat Transform:** This is a series of events hosted by VentureBeat, exploring the latest trends and challenges in technology and innovation.

- **ISG Future of Work Summit:** This summit is hosted by ISG, offering a range of sessions and workshops, including keynotes, peer-to-peer discussions, and expert-led sessions focused on the future of work and how technology is shaping it.

Each of these events offers a variety of opportunities for companies to engage with analysts, including keynote sessions, panel discussions, workshops, and networking opportunities. The specific offerings can vary by event, but the goal of these events is to provide companies with the latest insights and intelligence on technology, trends, and market challenges.

2.2 How Analysts and Research Firms Work

Analysts are an essential resource for technology companies, providing valuable insights into market trends, competitive activity, and the overall landscape. They play a crucial role in decision-making processes, strategic planning, and product development, making it essential for companies to build strong relationships with them.

So, how exactly do analysts work? First and foremost, analysts are information gatherers. They spend their days researching and analyzing various data sources, including industry reports, financial statements, customer surveys, and market research. They use this information to develop insights and recommendations that help companies make informed decisions.

Analysts also engage in a lot of networking. They attend industry events, speak with executives and experts, and maintain relationships with key stakeholders. Their goal is to stay up-to-date on the latest trends, news, and developments in their industry so that they can provide accurate and timely insights to their clients.

In addition to gathering information and networking, analysts also spend a lot of time writing reports and creating presentations. These materials are typically used by their clients to inform business decisions and communicate with stakeholders. Analysts must be skilled communicators and able to present complex information in a clear and concise manner.

Finally, analysts are often called upon to provide guidance and advice to their clients. This may involve helping them navigate a complex regulatory environment, identify new growth opportunities, or assess the feasibility of a new product or service.

To build strong relationships with analysts, it's essential to understand how they work and what motivates them. Analysts are driven by a desire to provide valuable insights and help their clients succeed. They value honesty, transparency, and responsiveness, and expect companies to be willing to listen to their recommendations and take them seriously.

By working closely with analysts, companies can gain a competitive edge and stay ahead of industry trends. Building strong relationships with analysts requires patience, persistence, and a willingness to engage in open and honest communication. With the right approach, companies can build lasting relationships with analysts and reap the rewards that come with their insights and recommendations.

2.3 Understanding their Research Process

For technology companies, building a strong relationship with analysts is crucial. Analysts can provide valuable insights into market trends, competitive intelligence, and customer needs. But to build a successful relationship with analysts, it's essential to understand their research process.

The research process of analysts typically involves three phases: discovery, analysis, and reporting. In the discovery phase, analysts gather data through various channels such as surveys, interviews, and secondary research. They use this data to identify market trends, customer needs, and competitive landscape.

In the analysis phase, analysts analyze the data they've gathered and use various tools and models to make sense of it. They identify patterns and trends, develop hypotheses, and test them against the data. This process involves a significant amount of data analysis, statistical modeling, and qualitative research.

In the reporting phase, analysts communicate their findings to their clients through various channels such as reports, webinars, and presentations. They provide recommendations and insights based on their analysis and help their clients make informed decisions.

To build a strong relationship with analysts, it's important to understand their research process and provide them with the resources they need to conduct their research effectively. This includes providing access to data, subject matter experts, and product information. It also involves building a relationship of trust and transparency, where analysts feel comfortable sharing their findings and recommendations.

Another key to building a successful relationship with analysts is to engage with them regularly. This includes attending industry events, participating in webinars, and providing feedback on their research. By staying engaged with analysts, you can build a rapport and develop a deeper understanding of their research process.

In summary, understanding the research process of analysts is critical to building a successful relationship with them. By providing them with the resources they need, engaging with them regularly, and building a relationship of trust and transparency, you can develop a strong and productive partnership with analysts.

CHAPTER 3

BUILDING STRONG RELATIONSHIPS WITH ANALYSTS

In the world of technology, building strong relationships with influencers is crucial for success. Analysts, journalists, and other tech influencers can help spread the word about your products and services, provide valuable feedback, and even influence your company's strategy. That's why relationship building is such an important part of any analyst relations strategy.

One of the key benefits of relationship building is that it helps you establish trust with influencers. When you take the time to get to know an analyst or journalist and build a rapport with them, they're more likely to trust you and your company. This can lead to more positive coverage and reviews, as well as a better understanding of your products and services.

Another benefit of relationship building is that it can help you get valuable feedback from influencers. Analysts and journalists often have a deep understanding of the technology industry and can offer insights that you might not have considered. By building a relationship with an influencer, you can get access to this valuable feedback and use it to improve your products and services.

Relationship building can also help you influence influencers. By building a strong relationship with an analyst or journalist, you can help shape their perception of your company and its products. This can lead to more positive coverage and reviews, as well as a better understanding of your company's strategy and goals.

Finally, relationship building can help you stay top-of-mind with influencers. When you regularly reach out to analysts and journalists, you ensure that your company is always on their radar. This can lead to more coverage and reviews, as well as more opportunities to collaborate on projects and events.

Overall, relationship building is a crucial part of any analyst relations strategy. By taking the time to get to know influencers and build a rapport with them, you can establish trust, get valuable feedback, influence perceptions, and stay top-of-mind. If you're a product marketing, analyst relations manager, PR manager, or influencer relationship manager, investing in relationship building can help you achieve your goals and drive success for your company.

Here are some tips for building strong relationships with analysts:

- **Communication is the Key:** Regular, open and honest communication is essential for building strong relationships. Keep analysts informed about your organization's activities, plans and results. Respond to their inquiries in a timely manner and provide them with the information they need to do their jobs effectively.

- **Be Transparent:** Analysts appreciate transparency, so don't be afraid to share information about your organization's strengths and weaknesses. This will help to build trust and credibility with the analyst community.

- **Provide Relevant Information:** Analysts need accurate and relevant information to do their jobs effectively. Make sure you provide them with information that is relevant to their area of expertise and that they can use in their analysis.

- **Build Personal Relationships:** Building personal relationships with analysts can help to strengthen your organization's relationship with them. Attend industry events, conferences and other networking opportunities where you can meet and connect with analysts.

✔ **Listen to Their Feedback:** Analysts can provide valuable insights and feedback on your organization's performance. Listen to their feedback and respond in a constructive manner. This will help to build trust and credibility with the analyst community.

Examples:

- A technology company regularly hosts analyst briefings to provide updates on its product portfolio and technology roadmap. The company also invites analysts to its product demonstrations and provides them with one-on-one time with its executives.

- A financial services company invites analysts to its annual investor conference, where they can hear about the company's strategy, performance, and future plans. The company also provides regular updates on its financial results and organizes conference calls with its senior executives.

- A consumer goods company invites analysts to tour its manufacturing facilities and meet with its senior management team. The company also provides regular updates on its market trends, consumer insights, and business results.

3.1 Nurturing Analyst Relationships

Building strong relationships with analysts should be a priority for any technology company. Not only do they shape industry opinions and influence purchasing decisions, but they also provide valuable insights into market trends and customer needs. Therefore, it is crucial to invest time and effort into nurturing these relationships.

Here are some tips for nurturing analyst relationships:

✔ **Build trust:** Analysts need to trust you and your company before they can recommend your products or services to their clients. Be transparent about your company's strengths and weaknesses, and provide them with accurate information. It is also essential to deliver on promises and commitments.

- ✔ **Understand their needs:** Analysts have specific research areas and interests. Take the time to understand their focus areas and tailor your communication and engagement accordingly. Make sure you are providing them with the information and resources they need to do their job effectively.

- ✔ **Provide value:** Analysts are busy professionals, and they receive a lot of information from various sources. To stand out, you need to provide them with valuable insights and information. Share your company's latest research, customer success stories, and industry trends that align with their interests.

- ✔ **Engage regularly:** Don't wait until you need something from analysts to engage with them. Regularly update them on your company's progress, and invite them to events and webinars. This will help build a relationship beyond the transactional level.

- ✔ **Listen and learn:** Analysts are experts in their field, and they can provide valuable feedback and insights. Listen to their opinions and ask for their feedback. This will help you understand their perspective and improve your products and services.

In conclusion, nurturing analyst relationships requires effort, time, and a willingness to listen and learn. Building trust, providing value, and engaging regularly are key to developing strong relationships with analysts. By investing in these relationships, you can gain valuable insights, increase your brand awareness, and ultimately drive business success.

Chapter 4

DEVELOPING A COMPREHENSIVE AR PLAN

An effective analyst relations (AR) plan is an essential component of a successful communication strategy. A comprehensive AR plan helps organizations to build relationships with the analyst community, promote their products and services, and increase visibility and credibility in the market.

Here are the steps to develop a comprehensive AR plan:

1. **Define Objectives:** Start by defining the goals and objectives of your AR program. What do you hope to achieve through your relationship with analysts? Do you want to increase visibility and credibility in the market, promote your products and services, or build relationships with the analyst community?

2. **Identify Key Analysts:** Determine which analysts are most relevant to your organization and prioritize your efforts accordingly. This may involve researching analyst firms, reading analyst reports and attending industry events to meet and connect with analysts.

3. **Develop Messaging:** Create a clear, consistent and compelling message that articulates your organization's value proposition and differentiates it from competitors. Ensure that your messaging is relevant to the needs and interests of the analyst community.

4. **Establish Communication Channels:** Determine the most effective ways to communicate with analysts, including regular briefings, conference calls, and in-person meetings. Make sure that the communication channels you establish are consistent with your overall communication strategy and support your goals and objectives.

5. **Plan Content:** Develop a content plan that includes relevant information, such as product updates, market trends, and thought leadership articles. Ensure that the content is relevant to the needs and interests of the analyst community and supports your messaging.

6. **Measure Results:** Regularly track and measure the success of your AR program. This may involve monitoring analyst coverage and feedback, tracking the impact of your content, and measuring the results of your analyst events and briefings.

Examples:

- A software company develops a comprehensive AR plan that includes regular analyst briefings, in-person meetings, and a content plan that features thought leadership articles and product updates. The company also establishes a regular process for monitoring analyst coverage and feedback.

- A financial services company creates an AR plan that includes regular conference calls with its senior executives, in-person meetings with key analysts, and a content plan that features market insights and thought leadership articles. The company also tracks the results of its AR program by monitoring analyst coverage and feedback.

- A technology company develops an AR plan that includes regular analyst briefings, in-person meetings, and a content plan that features thought leadership articles, product updates, and market trends. The company also establishes a regular process for monitoring analyst coverage and feedback and regularly tracks the results of its AR program.

The most important part is to know the publication calendar of the analyst and past reports. But one question will always be asked if you leading as AR team i.e. how do you determine an analyst relations budget which again can be a complex process as it involves considering various factors such as company size, industry, target markets, and goals for the analyst relations program.

Here are some steps that can be followed when deciding on an analyst relations budget:

1. **Assess the current state of the analyst relations program**: Look at what has worked well in the past and what needs improvement. This will help determine what resources are required to achieve the desired outcomes.

2. **Set goals and objectives:** Determine what the company hopes to achieve with its analyst relations program, such as improving market visibility, increasing product adoption, or enhancing the company's reputation.

3. **Research industry standards**: Research other companies in your industry and see how much they allocate for their analyst relations programs. This will give you a general idea of what a typical budget looks like.

4. **Consider internal resources:** Determine if you have internal resources, such as marketing and communications, that can assist with analyst relations initiatives. This can help reduce the budget needed for outside resources.

5. **Allocate budget based on priorities:** Decide which initiatives are the most important and allocate budget accordingly. This can include events, research projects, and travel expenses.

6. **Review and adjust regularly**: Analyze the results of the analyst relations program regularly and adjust the budget accordingly. This will ensure that resources are being used effectively and that the company is on track to achieve its goals.

It is important to remember that the analyst relations budget is not a one-time investment but an ongoing expense that should be reviewed and adjusted regularly. The budget should be flexible enough to accommodate changes in the market and the company's priorities.

4.1 Bridging the Gap: Building Relationships with Analysts

In today's fast-paced business world, building strong relationships with key analysts is essential for any technology company. These analysts are the gatekeepers to the industry, and their opinion can make or break a company's reputation. Bridging the gap between your company and these analysts is not always easy, but it is a necessary step in building a successful business.

The first step in building a relationship with an analyst is to do your research. You need to know who they are, what they cover, and what their interests are. This information can be found by reading their reports, following them on social media, and attending their events. Once you have this information, you can tailor your approach to match their interests and needs.

The second step is to reach out and introduce yourself. This can be done through email, phone, or in-person meetings. When reaching out, it is important to be brief and to the point. You should clearly state who you are, what your company does, and why you are interested in building a relationship with them. It is also important to be respectful of their time and to offer something of value in exchange for their attention.

Once you have established a relationship with an analyst, it is important to maintain it. This can be done by providing them with regular updates on your company and its products, as well as by offering them exclusive access to new products and features. It is also important to be responsive to their requests for information and to offer them opportunities to speak with your company's executives and product experts.

In conclusion, building strong relationships with key analysts is an essential part of managing analyst relations for technology companies. By doing your research, reaching out, and maintaining the relationship, you can bridge the gap between your company and these influencers and build a successful business. So, start building those relationships today and see how they can benefit your company.

4.2 Understanding and Implementing ENHANCE FRAMEWORK FOR IMPROVED AR

To help my audience and the broader team, I have created this **ENHANCE Framework** that helps people remember the basics of improving Analyst Relationship and also helps various team to be on the same page as it's an acronym that can be remembered easily.

E - Establish Clear Objectives

- Define your objectives for the Analyst Relations program, such as enhancing brand reputation, increasing market visibility, or improving analyst perceptions.

- Align your objectives with the overall business goals and strategies of your GSI.

- Ensure that your objectives are specific, measurable, achievable, relevant, and time-bound (SMART).

N - Nurture Relationships

- Build and maintain strong relationships with key analysts at the Analyst company.

- Engage in regular communication, including briefings, inquiries, and updates.

- Provide analysts with relevant and timely information about your GSI's capabilities, services, and industry insights.

- Seek opportunities to collaborate on research projects, whitepapers, or events.

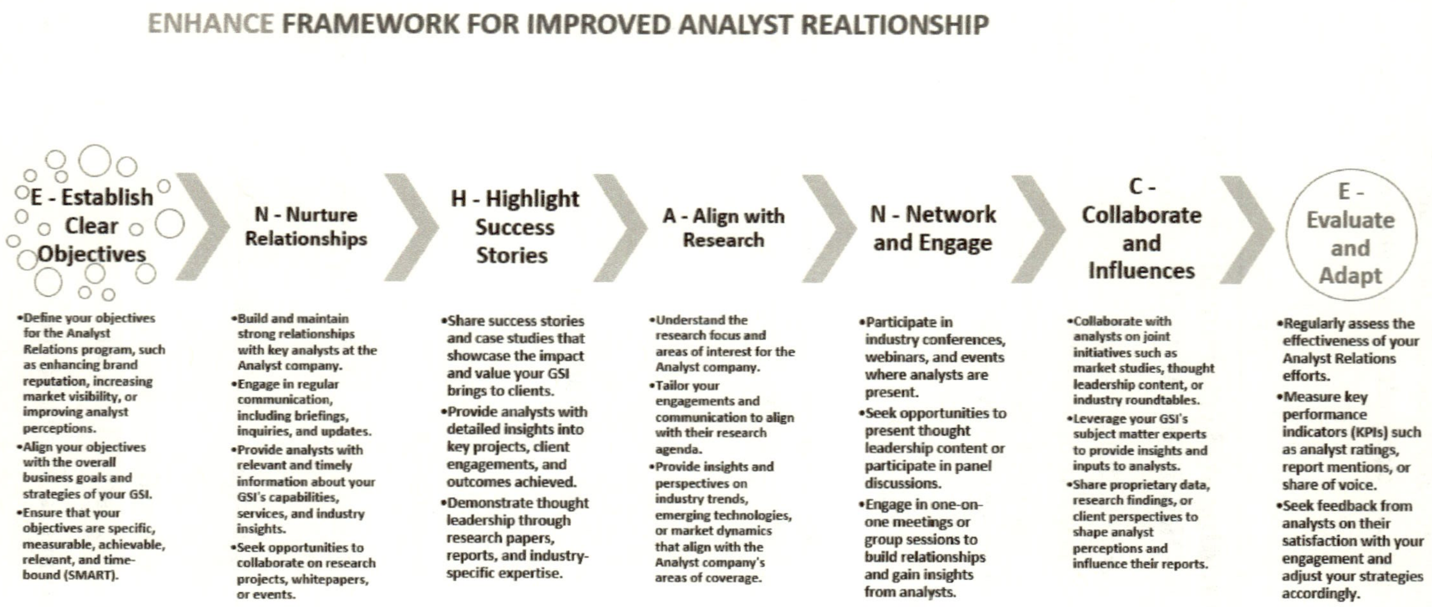

ENHANCE FRAMEWORK FOR IMPROVED ANALYST REALTIONSHIP

E - Establish Clear Objectives

- Define your objectives for the Analyst Relations program, such as enhancing brand reputation, increasing market visibility, or improving analyst perceptions.
- Align your objectives with the overall business goals and strategies of your GSI.
- Ensure that your objectives are specific, measurable, achievable, relevant, and time-bound (SMART).

N - Nurture Relationships

- Build and maintain strong relationships with key analysts at the Analyst company.
- Engage in regular communication, including briefings, inquiries, and updates.
- Provide analysts with relevant and timely information about your GSI's capabilities, services, and industry insights.
- Seek opportunities to collaborate on research projects, whitepapers, or events.

H - Highlight Success Stories

- Share success stories and case studies that showcase the impact and value your GSI brings to clients.
- Provide analysts with detailed insights into key projects, client engagements, and outcomes achieved.
- Demonstrate thought leadership through research papers, reports, and industry-specific expertise.

A - Align with Research

- Understand the research focus and areas of interest for the Analyst company.
- Tailor your engagements and communication to align with their research agenda.
- Provide insights and perspectives on industry trends, emerging technologies, or market dynamics that align with the Analyst company's areas of coverage.

N - Network and Engage

- Participate in industry conferences, webinars, and events where analysts are present.
- Seek opportunities to present thought leadership content or participate in panel discussions.
- Engage in one-on-one meetings or group sessions to build relationships and gain insights from analysts.

C - Collaborate and Influences

- Collaborate with analysts on joint initiatives such as market studies, thought leadership content, or industry roundtables.
- Leverage your GSI's subject matter experts to provide insights and inputs to analysts.
- Share proprietary data, research findings, or client perspectives to shape analyst perceptions and influence their reports.

E - Evaluate and Adapt

- Regularly assess the effectiveness of your Analyst Relations efforts.
- Measure key performance indicators (KPIs) such as analyst ratings, report mentions, or share of voice.
- Seek feedback from analysts on their satisfaction with your engagement and adjust your strategies accordingly.

H - Highlight Success Stories

- Share success stories and case studies that showcase the impact and value your GSI brings to clients.

- Provide analysts with detailed insights into key projects, client engagements, and outcomes achieved.

- Demonstrate thought leadership through research papers, reports, and industry-specific expertise.

A - Align with Research Areas

- Understand the research focus and areas of interest for the Analyst company.

- Tailor your engagements and communication to align with their research agenda.

- Provide insights and perspectives on industry trends, emerging technologies, or market dynamics that align with the Analyst company's areas of coverage.

N - Network and Engage

- Participate in industry conferences, webinars, and events where analysts are present.

- Seek opportunities to present thought leadership content or participate in panel discussions.

- Engage in one-on-one meetings or group sessions to build relationships and gain insights from analysts.

C - Collaborate and Influences

- Collaborate with analysts on joint initiatives such as market studies, thought leadership content, or industry roundtables.

- Leverage your GSI's subject matter experts to provide insights and inputs to analysts.

- Share proprietary data, research findings, or client perspectives to shape analyst perceptions and influence their reports.

E - Evaluate and Adapt

- Regularly assess the effectiveness of your Analyst Relations efforts.

- Measure key performance indicators (KPIs) such as analyst ratings, report mentions, or share of voice.

- Seek feedback from analysts on their satisfaction with your engagement and adjust your strategies accordingly.

By following the **ENHANCE framework,** you can develop a robust Analyst Relations program to improve the relationship between your GSI and the Analyst company. It involves establishing clear objectives, nurturing relationships, highlighting success stories, aligning with research areas, networking and engaging, collaborating and influencing, and continually evaluating and adapting your approach.

CHAPTER 5

CRAFTING EFFECTIVE COMMUNICATIONS FOR ANALYST OUTREACH

An effective analyst outreach program is an essential component of a comprehensive AR plan. By crafting effective communications for analyst outreach, organizations can build strong relationships with the analyst community and increase their visibility and credibility in the market.

Here are some preparations needed to craft effective communications for analyst outreach:

- **Identify Your Target Audience**: Determine which analysts are most relevant to your organization and prioritize your outreach efforts accordingly. Understanding the needs and interests of your target audience will help you to create relevant and compelling communications.

- **Develop a Consistent Messaging:** Create a clear, consistent and compelling message that articulates your organization's value proposition and differentiates it from competitors. Ensure that your messaging is relevant to the needs and interests of the analyst community.

- ✔ **Conduct Research:** Research the analyst firms, read their reports and articles, and understand their research areas of focus. This information will help you to tailor your outreach efforts and create relevant communications that support your goals and objectives.

Different ways to craft effective communications for analyst outreach:

- ✔ **Briefings:** Regular analyst briefings are an excellent way to provide updates on your organization's activities, plans and results. These briefings can take place in person, over the phone or through webinars.

- ✔ **Content:** Developing relevant and compelling content, such as thought leadership articles, market insights, and product updates, can help to build relationships with the analyst community. This content can be shared through email, social media, or your organization's website.

- ✔ **Events:** Hosting analyst events, such as product demonstrations or industry conferences, can help to build relationships with the analyst community and increase visibility and credibility in the market.

Different channels to reach analysts:

- ✔ **Email:** Email is a cost-effective and efficient way to reach analysts. Consider creating a targeted email campaign that includes relevant and compelling content.

- ✔ **Social Media:** Social media platforms, such as LinkedIn, Twitter and Facebook, can be used to reach analysts and build relationships with the analyst community. Consider sharing relevant and compelling content on these platforms.

- ✔ **Conferences:** Attending industry events and conferences is an excellent way to meet and connect with analysts. Consider sponsoring or speaking at events to increase your organization's visibility and credibility in the market.

- ✔ **Direct Outreach:** Direct outreach, such as one-on-one meetings or conference calls, can be an effective way to build relationships with analysts. Consider scheduling regular direct outreach with key analysts to ensure that your organization stays top-of-mind.

- ✔ **Research Portal:** Many major research providers like Gartner, Forrester and HFS provide a partner portal which can be purchased not only to read the latest technology report but also to raise a call also known as a 30 mins inquiry call with the analyst by filling a simple form within this portal.

5.1 How to <u>Connect</u> with Analysts

As a product marketing, analyst relations manager, PR manager, or influencer relationship manager, you know how important it is to build strong relationships with industry analysts. Analysts can help you gain valuable insights into your market, provide third-party validation for your products and services, and even influence purchasing decisions for potential customers.

But how do you connect with analysts in a meaningful way?

Here are some tips on how to connect with analysts:

1. **Do your research:** Before reaching out to an analyst, do your research on their areas of expertise and recent reports. This will help you tailor your message and show that you respect their time and insights.

2. **Attend industry events:** Analysts often attend industry events, conferences, and trade shows. Take advantage of these opportunities to meet them in person, introduce yourself, and learn more about their work.

3. **Build a relationship over time:** Don't expect to build a relationship with an analyst overnight. It takes time and effort to establish trust and rapport. Keep in touch with regular updates and invitations to events or webinars.

4. **Respect their time:** Analysts are busy people, so make sure to respect their time and schedule. When requesting a meeting or call, be clear about the purpose and agenda.

5. **Provide value:** Analysts are always looking for new insights and perspectives. Provide them with valuable information and data that they can use in their research and reports.

6. **Be transparent:** Analysts expect transparency and honesty from the companies they work with. Be transparent about your company's strengths and weaknesses, and don't try to hide or downplay any issues.

7. **Follow up:** After a meeting or call, make sure to follow up with a thank you note or email. This shows that you appreciate their time and insights.

By following these tips, you can build strong relationships with analysts and gain valuable insights into your market and industry. Remember, analysts are people, too, so treat them with respect and build a relationship over time. With a little effort and persistence, you can become an analyst whisperer and build strong relationships with tech influencers.

In conclusion, crafting effective communications for analyst outreach requires a clear understanding of your target audience, consistent messaging, and research. By using a combination of analyst briefings, content, events, and different channels, organizations can build strong relationships with the analyst community and increase their visibility and credibility in the market

5.2 How to Build an Effective Analyst Relations Program

Building an effective analyst relations program is crucial for technology companies to stay ahead of the competition and gain market share. Analysts play a critical role in shaping the perception of a company in the market, and having a strong relationship with them can help companies gain credibility, visibility, and valuable insights.

Here are some steps to build an effective analyst relations program:

1. **Define your goals:** Start by defining your objectives for the analyst relations program. Identify the key analysts that matter to your business and determine how you want to engage with them. Set clear metrics to measure the success of the program.

2. **Build a targeted list of analysts:** Identify the analysts that cover your industry and focus on those who have the most influence in your target market. Create a targeted list of analysts and prioritize them based on their relevance to your business.

3. **Develop a messaging framework:** Develop a messaging framework that resonates with the analysts and aligns with your company's strategy. Ensure that your messaging is consistent across all channels and communications.

4. **Engage with analysts regularly:** Build a relationship with the analysts by engaging with them regularly. Provide them with relevant information, insights, and access to key executives in your company. Make sure that you are responsive to their requests and provide them with timely and accurate information.

5. **Provide value to the analysts:** Provide the analysts with value by giving them access to your company's research, thought leadership, and product roadmap. Give them exclusive insights into your company's strategy and vision.

6. **Measure the impact of your program:** Measure the success of your analyst relations program by tracking the analyst coverage, mentions, and recommendations. Use the metrics to refine your program and improve your engagement with the analysts.

In conclusion, building an effective analyst relations program requires a strategic approach, targeted engagement, and a focus on providing value to the analysts. By following these steps, technology companies can build strong relationships with analysts, gain valuable insights, and enhance their reputation in the market.

Notes

CHAPTER **6**

MANAGING ANALYSTS DURING PRODUCT LAUNCHES AND MAJOR ANNOUNCEMENTS

Product launches and major announcements are significant events for organizations and require careful preparation and management of the analyst community. These events can impact an organization's reputation, visibility, and credibility in the market and, ultimately, its sales and revenue.

Here are some preparations needed to manage analysts during product launches and major announcements:

- ✔ **Plan Ahead:** Plan well in advance of the launch or announcement to ensure that you have sufficient time to prepare and communicate with the analyst community. Consider engaging with analysts early in the product development process to gain their insights and perspectives.

- ✔ **Develop a Clear Communication Plan**: Develop a clear communication plan that outlines the key messages and the target audience for each message. Ensure that your communication plan is consistent with your organization's overall messaging and brand strategy.

- ✔ **Identify Key Analysts:** Identify the key analysts who are relevant to your product launch or major announcement and prioritize your outreach efforts accordingly. Consider inviting key analysts to product demonstrations or briefings to gain their insights and perspectives.

- ✔ **Train Your Team:** Ensure that your team is trained and prepared to answer questions from the analyst community. Provide your team with a clear understanding of the key messages and the target audience for each message.

What can go wrong if not done right:

- **Miscommunication:** Miscommunication can lead to misunderstandings and confusion among the analyst community. This can impact an organization's reputation and credibility in the market.

- **Lack of Relevance:** Failing to tailor your communications to the needs and interests of the analyst community can result in a lack of relevance and engagement. This can impact an organization's visibility and credibility in the market.

- **Insufficient Preparation:** Insufficient preparation can result in a lack of focus and clarity during product launches and major announcements. This can impact an organization's ability to effectively communicate with the analyst community and deliver key messages.

Impact on the companies:

- **Reputation:** Poorly managed product launches and major announcements can have a negative impact on an organization's reputation and credibility in the market. This can result in a loss of sales and revenue.

- **Visibility:** Failing to effectively communicate with the analyst community during product launches and major announcements can impact an organization's visibility and credibility in the market. This can result in a loss of opportunities to reach potential customers.

- **Market Perception**: Poorly managed product launches and major announcements can impact the market perception of an organization and its products. This can result in a loss of sales and revenue.

Here are a few examples of how organizations have effectively managed analysts during product launches and major announcements:

- **Apple Inc.:** Apple is known for its highly anticipated product launches and has been successful in managing analysts during these events. Prior to each launch, Apple invites key analysts to product demonstrations or briefings to provide them with an in-depth understanding of the product and its features. This helps to build a strong relationship with the analyst community and ensures that the analysts are well-informed about the product before its launch.

- **Microsoft Corporation:** Microsoft is another example of an organization that effectively manages analysts during product launches and major announcements. Microsoft often holds press events and media briefings for key analysts to provide them with a comprehensive understanding of its products and their features. This helps to build a strong relationship with the analyst community and ensure that analysts are able to effectively communicate Microsoft's key messages to their audiences.

- **Amazon.com, Inc.:** Amazon is known for its highly effective product launches and announcements. Amazon engages with the analyst community early in the product development process to gain their insights and perspectives. Amazon also provides analysts with in-depth briefings and demonstrations to ensure that they are well-informed about the product before its launch. This helps to build a strong relationship with the analyst community and ensures that Amazon's key messages are effectively communicated to the market.

Here are a few examples of failed product launches in which analysts were not managed well:

- **Blackberry Z10**: In 2013, Blackberry launched the Z10 smartphone with high expectations. However, the launch was not well received by the analyst community due to a lack of clear communication and insufficient preparation. The analysts were not provided with enough information about the product's features and benefits, which led to confusion and a lack of engagement from the analyst community. This impacted Blackberry's reputation and credibility in the market, and contributed to the decline of the company.

- **HP TouchPad:** In 2011, HP launched the TouchPad tablet with high expectations. However, the launch was not well received by the analyst community due to a lack of clear communication and insufficient preparation. The analysts were not provided with enough information about the product's features and benefits, which led to confusion and a lack of engagement from the analyst community. This impacted HP's reputation and credibility in the market and contributed to the decline of the TouchPad product line.

- **Google Glass**: In 2013, Google launched the Google Glass wearable device with high expectations. However, the launch was not well received by the analyst community due to a lack of clear communication and insufficient preparation. The analysts were not provided with enough information about the product's features and benefits, which led to confusion and a lack of engagement from the analyst community. This impacted Google's reputation and credibility in the market and contributed to the decline of the Google Glass product line.

These examples demonstrate the importance of managing analysts effectively during product launches and major announcements. By failing to engage with the analyst community and provide clear communication, organizations can negatively impact their reputation and credibility in the market, leading to a decline in sales and revenue.

In conclusion, managing analysts during product launches and major announcements requires careful preparation and a clear communication plan. By engaging with the analyst community early in the process, developing a clear communication plan, and training your team, organizations can effectively communicate their key messages and maintain their reputation, visibility and credibility in the market.

Notes

CHAPTER **7**

HANDLING NEGATIVE ANALYST COVERAGE

Negative analyst coverage can have a significant impact on an organization's reputation, visibility, and credibility in the market. Negative coverage can arise due to a variety of reasons, including product flaws, marketing missteps, or financial challenges. In this chapter, we will discuss how organizations can handle negative analyst coverage and mitigate its impact on their reputation and bottom line.

7.1 Example 1: Tesla Inc. (2017)

In 2017, Tesla faced negative analyst coverage due to production challenges with its Model 3 vehicle. The company missed its production targets, leading to negative commentary from analysts who were skeptical about Tesla's ability to deliver its products on time. In response to the negative coverage, Tesla CEO Elon Musk took to Twitter to defend the company, providing updates on production progress and addressing the concerns of analysts and investors. As a result of Musk's engagement, Tesla was able to turn the narrative around and regain the confidence of the analyst community.

7.2   Example 2: Amazon.com Inc. (2018)

In 2018, Amazon faced negative analyst coverage due to concerns about the company's spending and its impact on profits. Analysts were concerned about the company's investments in areas such as shipping and technology, and expressed doubts about its ability to generate returns on these investments. In response to the negative coverage, Amazon's CEO Jeff Bezos provided a comprehensive update on the company's strategy, addressing the concerns of the analyst community and demonstrating the company's commitment to long-term growth. This helped to mitigate the impact of the negative coverage and regain the confidence of the analyst community.

7.3   Example 3: Alphabet Inc. (2019)

In 2019, Alphabet faced negative analyst coverage due to concerns about its advertising business and its impact on the company's financial performance. Analysts were concerned about the growing competition in the digital advertising space and expressed doubts about Alphabet's ability to maintain its dominance in the market. In response to the negative coverage, Alphabet's CEO Sundar Pichai provided a comprehensive update on the company's advertising strategy, addressing the concerns of the analyst community and demonstrating the company's commitment to maintaining its leadership position in the market. This helped to mitigate the impact of the negative coverage and regain the confidence of the analyst community.

Solutions:

- ✔ **Address the concerns directly:** Organizations can address the concerns raised in negative analyst coverage directly by providing updates and information that addresses the issues raised. This can help to demonstrate the organization's commitment to addressing the concerns of the analyst community and can help to regain the confidence of the analyst community.

- ✔ **Engage with the analyst community:** Organizations can engage with the analyst community to build relationships and gain insights into their concerns.

This can help organizations to better understand the concerns of the analyst community and provide information that addresses these concerns.

- ✔ **Focus on long-term growth:** Organizations can focus on their long-term growth strategy, demonstrating their commitment to delivering value to their customers and shareholders over the long term. This can help organizations to mitigate the impact of negative analyst coverage and regain the confidence of the analyst community.

In conclusion, negative analyst coverage can have a significant impact on an organization's reputation, visibility, and credibility in the market. However, by addressing the concerns raised directly, engaging with the analyst community, and focusing on long-term growth, organizations can mitigate the impact of negative analyst coverage and regain the confidence of the analyst community.

7.4 Responding to Negative Analyst Feedback

As a product marketing, analyst relations manager, PR manager, or influencer relationship manager, dealing with negative feedback from analysts can be challenging. However, it is important to understand that negative feedback is not always a bad thing. It can provide valuable insights into areas of improvement and help you to refine your product messaging and strategy.

Here are some tips for responding to negative analyst feedback:

1. **Listen and acknowledge the feedback:** The first step is to listen carefully to what the analyst is saying and acknowledge their concerns. It is important to show that you are taking their feedback seriously and that you respect their opinion. Avoid becoming defensive or dismissive of their feedback as this can damage your relationship with them.

2. **Address the concerns:** Once you have listened and acknowledged the feedback, it is important to address the concerns raised by the analyst. Be open and transparent about your plans to address the issues and provide a timeline for when they can expect to see improvements. Keep them updated throughout the process to show that you are taking their feedback seriously.

3. **Refine your messaging:** Negative feedback can be an opportunity to refine your product messaging and strategy. Use the feedback to identify areas of weakness and adjust your messaging accordingly. This can help to position your product more effectively in the market and differentiate it from competitors.

4. **Take action:** Ultimately, the best way to respond to negative feedback is to take action. Use the feedback to drive improvements in your product and messaging, and demonstrate to the analyst that you are committed to addressing their concerns. This can help to build trust and strengthen your relationship with them.

In conclusion, responding to negative analyst feedback can be challenging, but it can also be an opportunity to improve your product and messaging. By listening carefully, addressing concerns, refining your messaging, and taking action, you can build stronger relationships with analysts and position your product for success.

7.5 Overcoming Challenges in Working with Analysts

Managing analyst relations can be a tricky business, and there are several challenges that product marketing, analyst relations managers, PR managers, and influencer relationship managers may face. In this subchapter, we will discuss some of the common challenges in analyst relations and how to overcome them.

1. **Limited Resources:** One of the most significant challenges in analyst relations is limited resources. Many technology companies have a small team dedicated to managing analyst relations, which can make it difficult to build and maintain relationships with a large number of analysts. This can lead to missed opportunities and a lack of visibility in the marketplace.

   To overcome this challenge, it is essential to prioritize your resources and focus on building strong relationships with the analysts who are most relevant to your business. This can be done by identifying the analysts who cover your industry and products and reaching out to them regularly with relevant information and updates.

2. **Lack of Understanding:** Another common challenge in analyst relations is a lack of understanding of the analyst's role. Many people in technology companies do not fully understand the value that analysts can bring to their business, which can lead to a lack of investment in analyst relations.

   To overcome this challenge, it is essential to educate your colleagues about the role of analysts and the value they can bring to your business. This can be done by sharing analyst reports and research with your colleagues and highlighting the insights and recommendations that can help to inform your product and marketing strategies.

3. **Difficulty in Measuring ROI:** Measuring the ROI of analyst relations can be challenging, as it is often difficult to track the impact of analyst reports and recommendations on your business. This can make it challenging to justify the investment in analyst relations to senior management.

   To overcome this challenge, it is essential to establish clear goals and metrics for your analyst relations program. This can include metrics such as the number of analyst interactions, the number of mentions in analyst reports, and the impact of analyst recommendations on sales and revenue.

4. **Managing Expectations:** Finally, managing expectations can be a significant challenge in analyst relations. Analysts receive a large number of requests for briefings and information from technology companies, and it can be challenging to stand out from the crowd.

   To overcome this challenge, it is essential to be clear about your objectives and what you hope to achieve from your analyst relations program. This can help to ensure that your interactions with analysts are focused and productive and that you are able to build strong relationships that deliver value over time.

In conclusion, managing analyst relations for technology companies can be challenging, but by prioritizing your resources, educating your colleagues, establishing clear goals and metrics, and managing expectations, you can build strong relationships with analysts that deliver value to your business over time.

7.6 How to Overcome Challenges in Analyst Relations

As a product marketing, analyst relations manager, PR manager, or influencer relationship manager for a technology company, you are likely to face a variety of challenges in maintaining positive and productive relationships with analysts. These challenges may include a lack of understanding of the analyst's perspective, different expectations and priorities, and miscommunications or misunderstandings.

However, by implementing a few key strategies, you can overcome these challenges and build strong relationships with tech influencers. Here are some tips to help you navigate the complex world of analyst relations:

1. **Understand the Analyst's Perspective:** To build strong relationships with analysts, it is important to understand their perspective. This means taking the time to research their areas of expertise, the types of companies they cover, and the trends and issues they are focused on. By understanding their perspective, you can tailor your outreach and messaging to align with their interests and needs.

2. **Build Trust through Transparency:** Trust is essential in any relationship, and this is especially true in analyst relations. To build trust with analysts, it is important to be transparent about your company's strengths and weaknesses, and to provide honest and accurate information about your products and services. This includes being upfront about any limitations or challenges your company may be facing, and providing clear and concise messaging that aligns with the analyst's interests and needs.

3. **Focus on the Long-Term Relationship:** Analyst relations is a long-term game, and it is important to focus on building a strong and sustainable relationship with analysts over time. This means investing in regular communication, providing timely and relevant information, and being genuinely interested in the analyst's perspective and feedback.

4. **Emphasize Value Creation:** To maintain strong relationships with analysts, it is important to emphasize the value that your company can provide to them. This means understanding their needs and priorities, and tailoring your messaging and outreach to demonstrate how your products and services can help them meet their goals.

In conclusion, building strong relationships with analysts is a key component of managing analyst relations for technology companies. By understanding the analyst's perspective, building trust through transparency, focusing on the long-term relationship, and emphasizing value creation, you can overcome the challenges of analyst relations and build productive and valuable partnerships with tech influencers.

7.7 Handling Tough Analysts

As a product marketing, analyst relations manager, PR manager, or influencer relationship manager, you will inevitably encounter difficult analysts. These are the analysts who are hard to please, who constantly challenge your product or company, and who seem to enjoy pointing out flaws or weaknesses. Handling these analysts can be challenging, but it is an important part of your job. Here are some tips for dealing with difficult analysts:

1. **Listen to their concerns:** Difficult analysts often have valid concerns or criticisms. Don't dismiss their feedback out of hand. Instead, listen to what they have to say and try to understand where they are coming from. Ask questions to clarify their concerns and make sure you fully understand their perspective.

2. **Stay calm and professional:** It can be tempting to get defensive or emotional when dealing with difficult analysts, but this is rarely productive. Instead, stay calm and professional, even if the analyst is being confrontational or aggressive. Remember that you are representing your company and that your behavior reflects on your credibility and professionalism.

3. **Address their concerns directly:** Once you understand the analyst's concerns, address them directly. Be honest and transparent about any issues or challenges and explain what your company is doing to address them. If there are no immediate solutions, be clear about what steps you are taking to address the issue in the future.

4. **Provide additional information or context:** Difficult analysts may be missing important information or context that would help them better understand your product or company. Provide additional information or context that can help them better understand your position or perspective. This could include data, case studies, customer testimonials, or other relevant information.

5. **Know when to disengage** *(even analyst like everyone has biases)* : Sometimes, despite your best efforts, you may not be able to satisfy a difficult analyst. In these cases, it may be best to disengage and focus on building relationships with other analysts who are more receptive to your message. Don't waste time and energy on analysts who are unlikely to be convinced.

In conclusion, handling difficult analysts is a challenging but important part of managing analyst relations for technology companies. By listening to their concerns, staying calm and professional, addressing their concerns directly, providing additional information or context, and knowing when to disengage, you can build stronger relationships with even the most challenging analysts.

7.8 Dealing with Analyst Misunderstandings

In the world of technology, analysts are key influencers who can make or break a company's reputation. As a product marketing, analyst relations manager, PR manager, or influencer relationship manager, your job is to maintain a positive relationship with these analysts. However, misunderstandings can happen, and it's important to know how to deal with them.

1. **Listen and understand their perspective:** When dealing with an analyst misunderstanding, it's important to first listen and understand their perspective. Take the time to hear them out and try to see things from their point of view. Don't interrupt or argue with them, but instead, ask questions to clarify their concerns.

2. **Address their concerns:** Once you understand their perspective, it's important to address their concerns. Be transparent and honest in your responses. If there is an issue, admit to it and work towards finding a solution. If there is a miscommunication, clarify your message and make sure they understand your point of view.

3. **Provide additional information:** Sometimes, misunderstandings can arise due to a lack of information. In this case, provide the analyst with additional information that can help them understand the situation better. This can include data, reports, or other relevant materials.

4. **Follow up:** After addressing the issue, it's important to follow up with the analyst to ensure that they are satisfied with the resolution. Keep the lines of communication open and continue to build a positive relationship with them.

5. **Learn from the experience:** Finally, it's important to learn from the experience. Take the time to reflect on what happened and identify ways to prevent similar misunderstandings from happening in the future. This can include improving communication, providing more information upfront, or taking a different approach with the analyst.

In conclusion, dealing with analyst misunderstandings can be challenging, but it's important to approach the situation with a positive attitude and a willingness to listen and understand. By addressing their concerns and providing additional information, you can work towards finding a solution and maintaining a positive relationship with these key influencers in the world of technology.

7.9 Rebuilding Analyst Relationships

Analyst relationships are a critical component of any technology company's success. The insights and recommendations provided by industry analysts can help shape product roadmaps, go-to-market strategies, and even company culture. But what happens when those relationships sour? Rebuilding analyst relationships takes time, effort, and a willingness to listen and learn. In this chapter, we'll explore strategies for repairing damaged analyst relationships and getting back on track.

Step 1: Acknowledge the Problem

The first step in rebuilding a damaged analyst relationship is acknowledging that there is a problem. This can be difficult, as it requires a level of self-awareness and humility that is often in short supply. However, ignoring the problem or hoping it will go away on its own is not a viable solution. Instead, take the time to reflect on why the relationship soured. Was it a miscommunication? A difference in expectations? A failure to deliver on promises? Whatever the cause, acknowledging it is the first step in finding a solution.

Step 2: Listen and Learn

Once you've acknowledged the problem, the next step is to listen and learn. This means actively seeking out feedback from the analyst and taking the time to understand their perspective. What did they think went wrong? What could have been done differently? What are their expectations for the future? By listening and learning, you demonstrate a willingness to put the relationship first and a commitment to making things right.

Step 3: Take Action

Listening and learning are essential, but they are only the first steps in rebuilding an analyst relationship. The next step is to take action. This may mean making changes to your product roadmap, adjusting your messaging, or rethinking your go-to-market strategy. Whatever the action is, it needs to be concrete, measurable and focused on addressing the root cause of the problem. By taking action, you show that you are committed to fixing the problem and rebuilding the relationship.

Step 4: Maintain Two-way Communication

Finally, it's essential to maintain communication with the analyst throughout the rebuilding process. This means keeping them informed of any changes or progress and asking for feedback along the way. By maintaining communication, you demonstrate a commitment to transparency, collaboration, and accountability.

Rebuilding analyst relationships takes time, effort, and a willingness to listen and learn. But with the right approach, it is possible to repair damaged relationships and build stronger, more productive partnerships with industry analysts.

Notes

CHAPTER **8**

MEASURING THE IMPACT OF AR EFFORTS

In order to determine the effectiveness of your analyst relations (AR) efforts, it is important to measure the impact of your AR program. This can help you to identify areas for improvement and make informed decisions about how to allocate resources and prioritize your AR activities. In this chapter, we will discuss the different ways to measure the impact of AR efforts and provide examples from real life.

8.1 Example 1: Microsoft Corporation (2018)

In 2018, Microsoft conducted a survey of its analyst community to measure the impact of its AR efforts. The survey covered areas such as the quality of Microsoft's interactions with analysts, the relevance of its communications, and the level of trust and confidence that analysts had in Microsoft. The results of the survey helped Microsoft to identify areas for improvement in its AR program and to prioritize its AR activities accordingly.

8.2 Example 2: Apple Inc. (2019)

In 2019, Apple conducted a comprehensive analysis of its analyst coverage to measure the impact of its AR efforts. The analysis included metrics such as the frequency and prominence of analyst coverage, the tone of the coverage, and the impact of analyst coverage on the company's reputation and share price. The results of the analysis helped Apple to understand the impact of its AR efforts on its reputation and bottom line, and to make informed decisions about how to allocate resources and prioritize its AR activities.

8.3 Example 3: Amazon.com Inc. (2020)

In 2020, Amazon conducted a review of its analyst briefings to measure the impact of its AR efforts. The review covered areas such as the quality of the briefings, the relevance of the information provided, and the level of engagement from the analyst community. The results of the review helped Amazon to identify areas for improvement in its AR program and to make informed decisions about how to allocate resources and prioritize its AR activities.

Steps for Measuring the Impact of AR Efforts:

- **Identify key metrics:** Determine the key metrics that you will use to measure the impact of your AR efforts. This may include metrics such as the frequency and prominence of analyst coverage, the tone of the coverage, and the level of trust and confidence that analysts have in your company.

- **Collect data:** Collect data on your key metrics through a variety of methods, such as surveys of the analyst community, reviews of analyst briefings, or analyses of analyst coverage.

- **Analyze the data:** Analyze the data to determine the impact of your AR efforts on your reputation and bottom line. This may involve comparing your performance to that of your competitors or benchmarking your performance against industry standards.

- **Take action:** Based on the results of your analysis, take action to improve your AR program. This may involve adjusting your AR strategy, investing in new AR initiatives, or reallocating resources to more effective AR activities.

In conclusion, measuring the impact of AR efforts is critical to understanding the effectiveness of your AR program and making informed decisions about how to allocate resources and prioritize your AR activities. By identifying key metrics, collecting data, analyzing the data, and taking action based on your results, you can ensure that your AR efforts are having the desired impact and delivering value to your organization.

8.4 Measuring the Success of Analyst Relations

Measuring the success of analyst relations is critical in determining the effectiveness of your outreach efforts. The primary goals of analyst relations are to build strong relationships with industry analysts and to influence their opinions and recommendations about your company, products, and services. To measure the success of your analyst relations efforts, you need to set clear objectives, establish metrics, and track your progress over time.

Objectives: The first step in measuring the success of analyst relations is to define your objectives. What do you want to achieve through your outreach efforts? Some common objectives include:

- Increasing analyst coverage and mentions

- Improving analyst perception and understanding of your company, products, and services

- Enhancing your company's reputation and thought leadership in the industry

- Generating positive analyst reports, reviews, and recommendations

- Influencing analyst rankings and evaluations

Metrics: Once you have established your objectives, you need to identify the metrics that will help you measure your progress towards achieving them. Some common metrics include:

- Number of analyst briefings and inquiries

- Number of analyst reports, mentions, and recommendations

- Quality of analyst coverage and perception (e.g., positive vs. negative)

- Share of voice and influence in the analyst community

- Impact on analyst rankings and evaluations (e.g., Gartner Magic Quadrant)

Tracking and Analysis: To track your progress towards your objectives and metrics, you need to establish a system for collecting and analyzing data. This can include:

- Tracking analyst interactions and feedback in a CRM or other database

- Monitoring analyst coverage and mentions through media monitoring tools

- Conducting surveys or interviews to gauge analyst perception and understanding

- Analyzing trends and patterns in analyst reports and evaluations

By regularly tracking and analyzing your data, you can identify areas of strength and weakness in your analyst relations program and make adjustments to improve your outcomes.

Measuring the success of analyst relations is essential for managing effective outreach efforts and building strong relationships with industry analysts. By setting clear objectives, establishing metrics, and tracking your progress over time, you can identify areas of improvement and make data-driven decisions to enhance your company's reputation and influence in the industry.

CHAPTER **9**

NAVIGATING ETHICS AND CONFLICTS OF INTEREST IN AR

In the course of developing and maintaining relationships with analysts, it is important to consider and manage ethical considerations and conflicts of interest. Ethical conduct and transparency are essential in building and maintaining trust and credibility with the analyst community. In this chapter, we will discuss the ethical considerations and conflicts of interest that can arise in AR and provide examples and solutions for resolving them.

9.1 Example 1: Conflict of Interest with Vendor

A common conflict of interest in AR can arise when a company has relationships with both analysts and vendors. For example, suppose a company is working with a vendor that is also a client of an analyst. In that case, it is important to be transparent about these relationships and to avoid any appearance of preferential treatment or bias. The best way to resolve this conflict of interest is to clearly communicate the relationship to the analyst and to take steps to ensure that the analyst's coverage is impartial and objective.

9.2 Example 2: Providing Inaccurate or Misleading Information

Another ethical consideration in AR is the responsibility to provide accurate and truthful information to analysts. Providing false or misleading information to analysts can damage the company's reputation and undermine the trust and credibility of the AR program. To resolve this issue, companies should have clear guidelines and training programs in place to ensure that all AR communications are accurate and truthful. In the event that inaccurate information is provided to an analyst, it is important to promptly correct the information and take steps to rebuild trust with the analyst.

9.3 Example 3: Confidential Information

A third ethical consideration in AR is the handling of confidential information. Companies often have access to sensitive or proprietary information that should not be shared with analysts. To resolve this issue, companies should have clear policies in place to govern the handling of confidential information and should train their AR teams on these policies. In the event that confidential information is inadvertently shared with an analyst, it is important to promptly rectify the situation and take steps to prevent future breaches of confidentiality.

Steps for Resolving Ethical Considerations and Conflicts of Interest in AR:

- ✔ **Establish clear guidelines:** Establish clear guidelines for ethical conduct and the management of conflicts of interest in AR. This may include guidelines for handling confidential information, providing accurate and truthful information to analysts, and managing relationships with vendors and clients.

- ✔ **Provide training:** Provide training for your AR team on ethical considerations and conflicts of interest in AR. This will help to ensure that all AR communications are handled in a transparent and ethical manner.

- ✔ **Monitor and review:** Regularly monitor and review your AR activities to identify and resolve any ethical considerations or conflicts of interest that may arise.

- ✔ **Take corrective action:** If an ethical consideration or conflict of interest is identified, take prompt and effective action to resolve the situation and maintain the integrity of your AR program.

In conclusion, navigating ethical considerations and conflicts of interest in AR requires careful attention and effective management. By establishing clear guidelines, providing training, monitoring and reviewing AR activities, and taking corrective action as needed, companies can maintain the integrity of their AR programs and build trust and credibility with the analyst community.

Notes

CHAPTER **10**

STAYING UP-TO-DATE ON AR BEST PRACTICES AND TRENDS

Analyst Relations (AR) is a critical aspect of any company's overall public relations and marketing strategy. It involves developing and maintaining positive relationships with industry analysts and influencers, who can play a significant role in shaping public opinion and perception of a company and its products.

However, the field of AR is constantly evolving, with new best practices and trends emerging regularly. In order to remain effective and competitive in the field of analyst relations, it is important to stay up-to-date on the latest AR best practices and trends. This can be achieved through a combination of ongoing education, research, and networking with peers in the industry. In this chapter, we will discuss the different sources and methods for staying up-to-date on AR best practices and trends.

Here are a few reasons why staying up-to-date on AR best practices and trends is essential for success:

- ✔ **Competitive Advantage:** By staying up-to-date on the latest AR best practices and trends, companies can gain a competitive advantage in the market. They can ensure that their AR program is effective, efficient, and in line with the latest industry standards.

✔ **Improved Relationships with Analysts:** Staying up-to-date on AR best practices and trends can help AR professionals develop and maintain positive relationships with industry analysts and influencers. They can understand the evolving needs and expectations of these stakeholders and adjust their AR strategies accordingly.

✔ **Better Use of Technology:** The field of AR is being transformed by new technologies, and staying up-to-date on AR best practices and trends can help companies take advantage of these new technologies. This can improve the efficiency and effectiveness of their AR program, as well as provide a more engaging experience for analysts and influencers.

Sources of AR Information and Best Practices:

✔ **Professional Associations:** Joining professional associations such as the Analyst Relations Council (ARC) or the Technology Public Relations Council (TPRC) can provide access to industry insights, best practices, and networking opportunities.

✔ **Industry Conferences:** Attending industry conferences such as the AR Summit or the TPRC Conference can provide opportunities to learn about the latest AR best practices, trends, and technologies.

✔ **AR Webinars and Workshops:** Participating in AR webinars and workshops can provide in-depth education and training on specific AR topics.

✔ **AR Blogs and Websites:** Reading AR blogs and websites such as The AR Chronicle or The AR Professionals can provide access to insights, best practices, and case studies from industry experts and peers.

✔ **AR Networks:** Joining AR networks and communities on LinkedIn or other social media platforms can provide opportunities to connect with peers and share information and insights on AR best practices and trends.

10.1 Paid and Free Information Sources:

There are a variety of both paid and free information sources available for staying up-to-date on AR best practices and trends. Some paid sources include industry conferences, webinars, and workshops, while free sources include AR blogs and websites, AR networks, and professional associations. Companies can choose the information sources that best meet their needs and budget. They may consider a combination of both paid and free sources for a well-rounded and comprehensive approach to AR education and training.

In conclusion, staying up-to-date on AR best practices and trends is an important aspect of developing and maintaining a successful AR program. By utilizing a combination of professional associations, industry conferences, AR webinars and workshops, AR blogs and websites, and AR networks, companies can stay informed on the latest AR best practices and trends and ensure that their AR program remains competitive and effective.

Notes

CHAPTER 11

BUILDING A HIGH-PERFORMING AR TEAM AND ENSURING ITS SUCCESS

In the dynamic technology industry, having a strong analyst relations team is crucial to the success of any organization. Analysts play a key role in shaping the perception of a company and its products or services in the market. A positive relationship with influential analysts can help companies gain visibility, credibility, and even competitive advantage.

A strong analyst relations team can help companies navigate the complex landscape of analyst firms, manage relationships with analysts, and leverage analyst insights to inform product development, marketing, and sales strategies. Here are some reasons why a strong analyst relations team is essential for technology companies:

1. **Increase Visibility and Credibility**: Analysts have a wide reach and influence in the tech industry. Positive analyst coverage can increase the visibility and credibility of a company and its products or services, leading to increased brand awareness and market share.

2. **Shape Perception:** Analysts have the power to shape market perception of a company and its products. A strong analyst relations team can work with analysts to ensure that the company's message is accurately represented in the market.

3. **Gain Competitive Advantage**: Analysts can provide valuable insights into the market and competitors. A strong analyst relations team can leverage this insight to inform product development, marketing, and sales strategies, giving the company a competitive advantage.

4. **Navigate the Landscape:** The analyst landscape is complex and constantly evolving. A strong analyst relations team can help companies navigate the landscape, identify key analysts, and build relationships with them.

5. **Manage Relationships**: Building and maintaining positive relationships with analysts is essential. A strong analyst relations team can manage these relationships, ensuring that analysts have access to the right information and resources to accurately represent the company.

In conclusion, a strong analyst relations team is essential for technology companies looking to increase visibility, shape perception, gain competitive advantage, navigate the landscape, and manage relationships with influential analysts. Building a strong analyst relations team requires a combination of strategic planning, relationship management skills, and understanding of the analyst landscape. By investing in a strong analyst relations team, technology companies can drive growth, build brand awareness, and gain a competitive edge in the market.

The size and composition of an AR team can vary depending on the size and complexity of the company, but typically, the following individuals are involved:

- **AR Director or Manager**: This person is responsible for overseeing the overall AR program and ensuring that it is aligned with the company's overall goals and objectives. They lead the AR team, develop the AR strategy, and ensure that the AR program is effectively executed.

- **AR Specialists or Coordinators**: These individuals are responsible for executing the day-to-day activities of the AR program. They manage relationships with individual analysts, organize analyst briefings, and track analyst coverage and feedback.

- **Marketing and Communications Team**: The marketing and communications team plays a critical role in the AR program. They work with the AR team to develop messaging and positioning for the company and its products, and ensure that the AR program is effectively integrated with other marketing and communications activities.

- **Product Management Team:** The product management team is responsible for providing product and market insights to the AR team, and ensuring that the AR program is aligned with product development and launch activities.

- **Technical Team:** The technical team provides technical expertise to the AR team and works with the AR team to develop product presentations and briefings for analysts.

Executive Team: The executive team provides strategic direction and support for the AR program and helps to ensure that the AR program is effectively integrated with other business initiatives.

In conclusion, the AR team is composed of individuals with a variety of skills and expertise, including public relations, marketing, and communications, as well as technical expertise in the company's industry and target market. Each person on the AR team plays an important role in ensuring that the AR program is effectively executed and that the company's goals and objectives are achieved.

11.1   How to Build an Effective Analyst Relations Team

Building an effective analyst relations team is crucial for technology companies to succeed in today's market. Analysts are key influencers in the industry and can make or break a company's reputation. To build a successful analyst relations team, companies need to focus on three key areas: hiring the right people, creating a strong strategy, and fostering relationships with analysts.

- ✔ **Hiring the Right People:** The first step in building an effective analyst relations team is hiring the right people. Companies need to look for individuals with a deep understanding of the industry, strong communication skills, and the ability to build relationships. Analyst relations managers should have experience working with analysts and a track record of successful relationships. They should also have a deep understanding of the company's products and services, as well as the industry as a whole.

- ✔ **Creating a Strong Strategy:** Once the right team is in place, companies need to develop a strong analyst relations strategy. This should include identifying key analysts in the industry and understanding their areas of focus and influence. Companies should also have a clear understanding of their own strengths and weaknesses, as well as their competitors in the market. The strategy should outline how the company plans to engage with analysts, what messages they want to convey, and how they plan to measure success.

- ✔ **Fostering Relationships with Analysts:** Finally, to build a successful analyst relations team, companies need to foster strong relationships with analysts. This means engaging with them regularly, providing them with relevant and timely information, and being responsive to their inquiries. It also means being honest and transparent with analysts, even when the news may not be positive. Companies that invest in building strong relationships with analysts will be better positioned to influence their perceptions and drive positive coverage.

In conclusion, building an effective analyst relations team is critical for technology companies to succeed in today's market. By focusing on hiring the right people, creating a strong strategy, and fostering relationships with analysts, companies can build a team that is well-positioned to influence the market and drive positive coverage.

11.2 Hiring the Right Analyst Relations Professionals

As technology companies strive to maintain their competitive edge, they recognize the importance of building strong relationships with industry analysts. Analyst relations professionals play a critical role in this process, as they are responsible for engaging with analysts, understanding their research areas, and positioning their company's products and services as the best in the market.

When it comes to hiring analyst relations professionals, there are a few key factors to consider. First, it's important to look for candidates with a deep understanding of the technology industry and the analyst landscape. This includes knowledge of the major research firms, as well as a strong understanding of the trends and challenges facing the industry.

Another key factor to consider is the candidate's relationship-building skills. Analyst relations professionals must be able to cultivate strong relationships with key analysts, which requires excellent communication skills and the ability to navigate complex organizations and personalities.

In addition, it's important to look for candidates with a strong strategic mindset. This includes the ability to develop and execute effective analyst relations plans, as well as the ability to measure the impact of those plans and adjust them as needed.

When interviewing candidates for analyst relations positions, it's also important to ask about their experience working with specific research firms and analysts. This can help you gauge their level of familiarity with the landscape and their ability to effectively engage with key influencers.

Overall, hiring the right analyst relations professionals is a crucial step in building strong relationships with industry analysts and positioning your company as a leader in the technology industry. By focusing on key skills, experience, and relationship-building abilities, you can find the right candidate to help take your analyst relations efforts to the next level.

11.3 Training Analyst Relations Professionals (Internal +External)

In today's digital age, the role of an analyst relations professional has become more critical than ever before. With the rise of tech influencers who can significantly impact a company's reputation and sales, it is essential to have a team of professionals who can build and maintain strong relationships with these experts. However, finding the right talent and ensuring their skills are up-to-date can prove challenging. This is where training comes in.

Training professionals in analyst relations is an essential component of effectively managing analyst relations within technology companies. To succeed in this role, individuals responsible for analyst relations (AR) should possess a comprehensive understanding of their organization's past engagements with analysts, an overview of the current state of interactions with the analyst community, as well as an in-depth knowledge of the internal capabilities of their solutions or products in comparison to competitors. Additionally, a clear grasp of the allocated AR budgets is paramount for successful planning and execution in this area.

It helps to ensure that the AR professional is well equipped with the necessary skills and knowledge to foster positive relationships with tech influencers. Here are some tips on how to train analyst relations professionals.

1. **Understand the role of an analyst relations professional:** Before training analyst relations professionals, it is essential to understand the role they play in the organization. An analyst relations professional is responsible for building and maintaining relationships with tech influencers such as analysts, journalists, and bloggers. They act as a bridge between the company and the tech influencers, providing them with relevant information and insights about the company's products and services.

2. **Develop a training program:** Develop a training program that covers the basics of analyst relations and the skills required to excel in the role. The training program should include modules on building relationships with tech influencers, managing expectations, and effectively communicating with them. It should also cover topics such

as understanding the analyst landscape, identifying key influencers, and tracking analyst coverage.

3. **Provide hands-on experience:** Providing hands-on experience is crucial in training analyst relations professionals. Please keep some budget aside for AIIR certification and product trainings. This can be achieved by assigning them to work on real-world projects and providing them with opportunities to interact with tech influencers. It is also essential to provide them with feedback and guidance to help them improve their skills.

4. **Encourage continuous learning:** Encourage continuous learning by providing access to industry events, webinars, and training programs. Please allocate some budget for AR professional to visit and learn from global events. This will help them stay up-to-date with the latest trends and developments in the industry and hone their skills.

In conclusion, training analyst relations professionals is crucial for managing analyst relations for technology companies. Here are some of the industry certifications available;

1. **Institute of Industry Analyst Relations (IIAR):** IIAR offers a certification program that's geared towards AR professionals. It's designed to help individuals develop the skills and knowledge required for success in the field of AR.

2. **APR (Accredited in Public Relations):** While not specific to AR, the APR certification from the Public Relations Society of America (PRSA) is valuable for PR and communication professionals, which often includes AR responsibilities.

3. **ARInsights Certification:** ARInsights, a company that provides tools and resources for AR professionals, offers a certification program. While not as widely recognized as some other certifications, it's focused specifically on analyst relations.

4. **Technology-specific training:** Many technology companies offer in-house training or workshops for their AR teams, which can be quite valuable for those in the technology sector. These may not be formal certifications but can be highly relevant.

5. **General PR and Communications Certifications**: While not AR-specific, certifications like the Chartered Institute of Public Relations (CIPR) and the International Association of Business Communicators (IABC) offer programs that can be beneficial for AR professionals.

By understanding the role of an analyst relations professional, developing a training program, providing hands-on experience, and encouraging continuous learning, companies can build a team of professionals who can effectively manage analyst relations and build stronger relationships with tech influencers.

Chapter 12

LEVERAGING SOCIAL MEDIA FOR ANALYST RELATIONS

In today's digital age, social media has revolutionized communication and networking, presenting valuable opportunities for analyst relations (AR) professionals. By effectively utilizing social media platforms, AR practitioners can enhance relationships with analysts, expand their reach, and strengthen their overall AR strategy. This chapter explores the importance of leveraging social media for analyst relations and provides practical insights on how to harness these platforms to build connections, share insights, and drive positive outcomes.

Understanding the Role of social media in Analyst Relations:

- Overview of key social media platforms relevant to AR, such as Twitter, LinkedIn, and industry-specific forums.

- Examples of successful AR initiatives leveraging social media to engage with analysts and share information.

- The evolving landscape of social media in the analyst community and its impact on traditional AR practices.

Examples of successful AR initiatives leveraging social media to engage with analysts and share information include:

- **Twitter Chats**: Hosting live Twitter chats where AR professionals and analysts come together to discuss industry trends, emerging technologies, and relevant topics. This interactive format allows for real-time engagement, exchange of ideas, and building relationships with analysts.

- **LinkedIn Thought Leadership:** AR professionals establishing a strong presence on LinkedIn by regularly sharing industry insights, research findings, and thought-provoking articles. This positions them as experts in their field and encourages analysts to engage with their content, leading to increased visibility and credibility.

- **Analyst Briefing Livestreams**: Broadcasting analyst briefings and product launches through live video streaming platforms like YouTube or Facebook Live. This enables analysts who may not be physically present to participate remotely and provides a wider audience with real-time updates and information.

- **Social Media Listening and Engagement**: Actively monitoring social media platforms to identify discussions, questions, or comments from analysts. Responding promptly and thoughtfully to these interactions demonstrates a commitment to engagement and fosters positive relationships with analysts.

- **Industry-Specific Forums and Communities**: Participating in and contributing to online forums or communities focused on specific industries or technologies. By sharing valuable insights, answering questions, and engaging in discussions, AR professionals can establish themselves as trusted resources and build rapport with analysts who frequent these platforms.

- **Webinars and Live Q&A Sessions**: Hosting webinars or live Q&A sessions on social media platforms to address industry-specific topics and allow analysts to ask questions directly. This interactive format fosters dialogue, enables knowledge sharing, and enhances engagement with analysts.

- **Visual Content and Infographics**: Creating visually appealing content, such as infographics or data visualizations, specifically designed for social media sharing. This helps capture analysts' attention, conveys complex information in a digestible format, and encourages them to engage with and share the content within their networks.

These examples illustrate how leveraging social media platforms effectively can facilitate meaningful interactions, expand reach, and strengthen relationships with analysts. By employing these strategies, AR professionals can enhance their overall analyst relations efforts and maximize the impact of their communication and engagement initiatives.

✔ **Developing a Social Media Strategy for Analyst Relations:**

   a. Defining clear objectives and goals for social media engagement in AR.

   b. Identifying target audiences and determining the most suitable social media platforms to reach them.

   c. Crafting a consistent and compelling social media presence that aligns with the AR strategy.

   d. Integrating social media activities into the overall AR plan to maximize impact and synergy.

✔ **Building Relationships with Analysts through Social Media:**

   a. Engaging in meaningful conversations and discussions with analysts on social media platforms.

   b. Showcasing industry expertise by sharing relevant news, insights, and research reports.

   c. Utilizing social media to request analyst feedback and encourage their active participation.

   d. Establishing thought leadership by creating and curating valuable content that resonates with analysts.

- **Amplifying Analyst Relations Activities through social media:**

  a. Live-tweeting or live-blogging analyst briefings and industry events to generate real-time engagement and visibility.

  b. Promoting analyst reports, positive coverage, and endorsements through social media channels.

  c. Encouraging analysts to share their perspectives and insights on social media platforms.

  d. Collaborating with analysts on joint content creation, such as guest blog posts or podcast episodes.

- **Monitoring and Managing Social Media Interactions:**

  a. Implementing tools and techniques to monitor social media conversations relevant to AR.

  b. Responding promptly to analyst inquiries, comments, and feedback on social media platforms.

  c. Addressing any negative sentiment or criticism professionally and transparently.

  d. Establishing guidelines and best practices for AR professionals' use of social media to maintain consistency and professionalism.

- **Measuring the Impact of Social Media on Analyst Relations:**

  a. Identifying key performance indicators (KPIs) to evaluate the effectiveness of social media efforts.

  b. Tracking engagement metrics, including reach, impressions, likes, shares, and comments.

c. Assessing the influence of social media activities on analyst relationships and coverage.

d. Incorporating social media insights into the overall measurement of AR performance and success.

Leveraging social media for analyst relations empowers AR professionals to enhance their interactions with analysts, expand their visibility, and drive positive outcomes. Real-world examples demonstrate how successful companies have effectively utilized social media to engage with analysts and amplify their AR initiatives. By understanding the role of social media, developing a comprehensive strategy, fostering meaningful relationships, and measuring impact, AR professionals can harness the power of these platforms to propel their efforts and achieve AR success in the digital age.

Notes

CHAPTER **13**

ENGAGING WITH ANALYSTS IN THE DIGITAL ERA

In the digital era, analyst relations (AR) professionals must adapt their strategies to effectively engage with analysts amidst the ever-changing technological landscape. This chapter delves into the considerations and best practices for engaging with analysts in the digital era, harnessing technology, and capitalizing on digital platforms to maximize opportunities.

13.1 Understanding the Digital Transformation of Analyst Relations:

The rise of digital technologies has profoundly impacted the analyst landscape, necessitating a shift in AR approaches. Analysts now have different expectations and rely heavily on digital channels for research and information gathering. AR professionals need to understand the influence of digital platforms on analysts' workflows and adapt their strategies accordingly. This includes recognizing the growing importance of virtual briefings, webinars, and remote interactions facilitated by digital platforms.

13.2   Building a Digital Engagement Strategy:

To successfully engage with analysts in the digital era, AR professionals must establish a robust digital engagement strategy. This involves defining clear objectives and goals for digital engagement, selecting the most appropriate digital platforms and channels for interaction, and crafting a comprehensive content strategy tailored to these platforms. Interactive elements such as polls, surveys, and Q&A sessions can be integrated to enhance engagement and foster two-way communication.

13.3   Leveraging social media for Analyst Engagement:

Social media platforms offer valuable opportunities for connecting with analysts, sharing industry insights, and fostering conversations. AR professionals can utilize these platforms to actively listen to and monitor analyst discussions, respond to queries, and participate in relevant conversations. By leveraging social media, AR professionals can position themselves as thought leaders and engage analysts in meaningful dialogue.

For example, a software company may engage with analysts by sharing their latest research findings on Twitter and inviting them to a live Q&A session.

13.4   Virtual Briefings and Webinars:

In the digital era, virtual briefings and webinars have become indispensable tools for engaging with analysts. AR professionals can conduct virtual briefings and presentations using video conferencing tools or dedicated webinar platforms. To ensure an engaging virtual experience, effective presentation techniques and interactive features can be employed. Virtual environments provide opportunities for showcasing product demonstrations, virtual tours, or interactive workshops.

For instance, a technology company might organize a webinar to present a new product release and invite analysts to join for an interactive session, allowing them to ask questions and provide feedback in real-time.

13.5 Digital Content Creation and Distribution:

Creating high-quality digital content tailored to analyst interests is crucial for effective engagement. AR professionals can develop whitepapers, e-books, and videos that provide valuable insights to analysts. Optimizing content for search engines enhances discoverability, maximizing organic reach to analysts. Content distribution platforms and email marketing can be utilized to share relevant content directly with analysts, increasing their exposure to valuable information.

13.6 Enhancing Analyst Relationships through Digital Engagement:

Digital engagement can play a vital role in building and nurturing relationships with analysts. Personalized and targeted digital communications contribute to rapport and trust. Regular virtual meetings and check-ins ensure consistent communication and foster strong relationships. Facilitating collaboration and knowledge sharing through shared digital workspaces, collaborative documents, and online forums further enhances engagement.

There is tremendous scope in using this aspect of analyst relations engagement along. For instance;

- **Personalized Digital Communications:** AR professionals can strengthen relationships with analysts by utilizing personalized digital communications. This can include sending personalized emails or direct messages to analysts, sharing relevant updates, industry insights, or exclusive content tailored to their specific interests. For example, an AR professional might reach out to an analyst directly on LinkedIn to share a recent research report that aligns with their area of expertise.

- **Virtual Meetings and Check-Ins:** In the digital era, AR professionals can schedule regular virtual meetings and check-ins with analysts to maintain consistent communication and foster rapport. These virtual meetings can be conducted using video conferencing tools, allowing for face-to-face interactions even when physical meetings are not feasible. By proactively scheduling these virtual engagements, AR professionals can demonstrate their commitment to building strong relationships and addressing any questions or concerns raised by analysts.

- **Collaboration through Shared Digital Workspaces:** Digital workspaces provide a platform for collaborative engagement between AR professionals and analysts. By leveraging shared digital workspaces such as project management tools or online document collaboration platforms, AR professionals can co-create content, share updates, and collaborate on joint initiatives with analysts. This collaborative approach fosters a sense of partnership and strengthens the relationship by involving analysts in the AR process.

- **Participation in Online Forums and Communities:** Engaging with analysts in online forums and industry-specific communities is an effective way to enhance relationships through digital channels. AR professionals can actively participate in relevant discussions, answer questions, provide insights, and offer assistance to analysts seeking information. By actively engaging in these digital communities, AR professionals position themselves as valuable resources and build credibility among analysts.

- **Webinar Q&A Sessions and Feedback:** When hosting webinars or virtual events, AR professionals can include interactive elements such as Q&A sessions to encourage analyst participation. By allowing analysts to ask questions, provide feedback, and engage in real-time dialogue, AR professionals can foster a deeper level of engagement and establish a collaborative relationship. Gathering and incorporating feedback from analysts after webinars or events further demonstrate a commitment to their insights and strengthens the bond between AR professionals and analysts.

These examples illustrate how AR professionals can enhance relationships with analysts through various digital engagement strategies. By utilizing personalized communication, virtual meetings, collaboration through shared workspaces, active participation in online communities, and incorporating interactive elements in webinars, AR professionals can build strong and meaningful relationships with analysts in the digital era.

13.6.1 Measurement and Evaluation of Digital Engagement:

To gauge the effectiveness of digital engagement efforts, it is essential to identify key performance indicators (KPIs) for measurement. Tracking engagement metrics such as views, downloads, social media interactions, and webinar attendance provides insights into the reach and impact of digital engagement. Analysis of these metrics helps evaluate the influence of digital engagement on analyst perception, coverage, and relationships.

But the biggest challenge is what those metrics are, as most of the analysts will tell you it is not about the quadrant, but the value lies in their critical advisory. However, he will have all the data of previous communication and can also know whether you're an AR portal subscriber or not. (yes, your AR subscription consumption is measure by these portals). However, any AR manger can monitor his or his team's performance using the following simple criteria; (quarter on quarter as per publication calendar)

- **Engagement Metrics:** AR professionals can track engagement metrics to assess the effectiveness of their digital engagement efforts. This can include measuring the number of views, likes, comments, and shares on social media platforms for content shared with analysts. By analyzing these metrics, AR professionals can gauge the level of interest and interaction generated by their digital engagement initiatives.

- **Webinar Attendance and Feedback:** For virtual events such as webinars, measuring the number of attendees and gathering feedback from analysts provides valuable insights into the impact of digital engagement. AR professionals can assess the level of participation, the quality of discussions, and the satisfaction of analysts through post-webinar surveys or feedback forms. This data can inform future webinar strategies and help refine the content and format to better engage analysts.

- **Content Downloads and Consumption:** Monitoring the number of downloads or views of digital content shared with analysts provides insights into the reach and impact of the content. AR professionals can track the download or view metrics for whitepapers, e-books, research reports, or other digital assets to determine the level of interest and engagement from analysts. By analyzing this data, AR professionals can identify which content resonates most with analysts and optimize future content creation efforts.

- **Analyst Sentiment Analysis:** AR professionals can employ sentiment analysis techniques to evaluate the sentiment expressed by analysts in their digital interactions. By using natural language processing tools, sentiment analysis can help determine whether analysts' responses, comments, or feedback are positive, neutral, or negative. This analysis provides valuable feedback on the overall perception of AR efforts and enables AR professionals to address any concerns or negative sentiment effectively.

- **Influencer and Reach Metrics:** AR professionals can leverage social media analytics tools to measure the reach and influence of their digital engagement initiatives. These tools can provide insights into the number of followers, impressions, and shares generated by AR content shared with analysts. By tracking these metrics, AR professionals can assess the effectiveness of their digital engagement in extending their reach and impacting the analyst community.

- **Analyst Coverage and Citations:** Another measure of the impact of digital engagement is the coverage and citations received from analysts. By monitoring analyst reports, articles, or mentions in industry publications, AR professionals can assess the influence of their digital engagement efforts on analysts' research and opinions. This provides a qualitative measure of the impact and recognition gained through digital engagement initiatives.

By measuring and evaluating these digital engagement metrics, AR professionals can gain valuable insights into the effectiveness, reach, and impact of their efforts. These insights enable them to refine their digital engagement strategies, optimize content creation, and make informed decisions to further enhance their engagement with analysts in the digital era.

Engaging with analysts in the digital era demands adaptability and a proactive approach from AR professionals. By embracing digital transformation, AR professionals can establish meaningful relationships, provide valuable insights, and collaborate effectively with analysts. Incorporating digital engagement into the AR strategy ensures relevance and effectiveness in a rapidly evolving technological landscape, ultimately driving positive outcomes and influencing the perception of industry analysts.

Notes

CHAPTER **14**

EFFECTIVE EVENT MANAGEMENT FOR ANALYST RELATIONS

Events serve as valuable platforms for engaging with industry analysts, sharing insights, and building relationships. This chapter explores the importance of event management in analyst relations and provides insights into planning, execution, success measurement, and examples of successful events organized by various companies.

- ✔ **Importance of Events in Analyst Relations:** Events play a significant role in analyst relations by providing opportunities for direct interaction, knowledge sharing, and relationship-building with analysts. Whether through analyst briefings, conferences, product launches, or virtual events, companies can showcase their offerings, address analyst queries, and garner support from influential industry experts.

- ✔ **Planning and Execution:** Successful event management requires meticulous planning and execution. This involves defining clear objectives for the event, identifying the target audience of analysts, and creating compelling content that aligns with the event's theme. Careful consideration should be given to logistics, including venue selection, catering, and budget allocation, to ensure a seamless experience for both the company and attending analysts.

- ✔ **Examples of Successful Events:** Real-world examples demonstrate the effectiveness of well-executed events in analyst relations. For instance, the Gartner Symposium/ITxpo organized by Gartner offers companies a platform to present their technology and network with analysts. Microsoft Ignite, Microsoft's annual conference, serves as a showcase for its latest products and strategic direction.

- ✔ **Event Management on a Limited Budget:** Companies with budget constraints can still effectively manage events in analyst relations. Virtual events, such as webinars or online conferences, provide cost-effective alternatives while allowing for engagement and knowledge sharing. Regional roundtable discussions offer a more focused and targeted approach, minimizing expenses associated with large-scale conferences.

- ✔ **Event Management with Ample Resources:** Companies with larger budgets can explore more extravagant event options. Exclusive retreats or destination events provide a luxurious and immersive experience for a select group of analysts, facilitating deeper engagement and relationship-building. Customized experiences, such as personalized agendas and executive meet-and-greets, offer tailored interactions that leave a lasting impression.

- ✔ **Measuring Event Success:** Evaluating the success of an event in analyst relations involves various metrics. Attendance and engagement indicators measure the number of analysts attending the event and their level of active participation. Gathering feedback from analysts through surveys or individual discussions provides valuable insights into the event's impact and perceived value. Monitoring media coverage and citations post-event offers an indication of its influence and reach. Additionally, assessing the return on investment (ROI) helps determine the overall value derived from the event by comparing costs with desired outcomes, such as increased analyst support, positive coverage, or generated leads.

Effectively managing events is crucial in analyst relations as they facilitate engagement, knowledge sharing, and relationship-building with industry analysts. Whether operating on a limited or ample budget, companies can leverage various strategies to create impactful experiences

Participating in analyst relationship (AR) events and conferences is a valuable way for AR professionals to engage with industry analysts, strengthen relationships, and gain insights into market trends. Here are some major AR events and conferences that AR professionals can participate in:

- **Gartner Symposium/ITxpo:** Gartner's Symposium/ITxpo events are among the largest and most influential gatherings in the tech industry. They offer opportunities for AR professionals to engage with Gartner analysts and get insights into technology trends.

- **Forrester Research Webinars and Conferences:** Forrester Research hosts various webinars, forums, and conferences throughout the year. These events provide a platform for AR professionals to connect with Forrester analysts.

- **IDC Directions:** IDC Directions events are held annually and provide insights into emerging technology trends. They are an excellent opportunity for AR professionals to connect with IDC analysts.

- **OpenWorld by Oracle:** Oracle's OpenWorld conference brings together technology professionals, including AR practitioners. It's an opportunity to connect with Oracle's own analysts and network with other professionals in the industry.

- **CIOsynergy:** CIOsynergy events provide a platform for AR professionals to engage with CIOs and IT decision-makers. These interactions can help in understanding the priorities and concerns of CIOs.

- **Institute of Industry Analyst Relations (IIAR) Events:** The IIAR hosts various events and webinars designed to support AR professionals and provide opportunities to connect with industry analysts.

- **Vendor-Specific Analyst Summits:** Many large technology companies, such as Microsoft, IBM, and Cisco, host their own analyst summits. These events are a great way for AR professionals to engage with both internal and external analysts.

- **ARchitect User Groups:** Some organizations, like ARInsights, host user group events where AR professionals can share best practices and learn from each other.

- **Local AR and PR Meetups:** Depending on your location, there may be local meetups and events for AR and PR professionals. These can be a great way to network and learn from peers.

Remember that participation in these events can vary in terms of cost and accessibility. Some may be open to anyone, while others may be invitation-only. By setting clear objectives, planning meticulously, and measuring success through attendance, engagement, feedback, media coverage, and ROI analysis, companies can optimize their event management efforts and maximize the impact of analyst relations events. It's important to plan your participation in advance and make the most of these opportunities to build and strengthen relationships with industry analysts, which is a crucial part of the AR role.

CHAPTER 15

MAXIMIZING ANALYST RELATIONS ROI

Maximizing return on investment (ROI) is crucial in analyst relations (AR) to ensure the effectiveness and value of initiatives. By implementing strategic approaches and evaluating outcomes, companies can optimize their AR efforts.

Measuring the return on investment (ROI) for Analyst Relations (AR) programs can be challenging due to the indirect and cumulative nature of the outcomes. However, there are several key performance indicators (KPIs) and metrics that AR professionals can use to gauge the effectiveness and impact of their efforts. Here are some common ways to measure the investment in AR, accompanied by examples for each:

- **Analyst Coverage and Mention**: Track the number of times your company or products are mentioned in reports, articles, or blog posts by industry analysts. For example, if your company's mentions in Gartner reports have increased by 30% over the year, it indicates a growing influence.

- **Analyst Recommendations**: Pay attention to any recommendations made by analysts regarding your company's products or services. If an influential analyst recommends your software as a top solution, this can have a direct impact on purchasing decisions.

- ✔ **Share of Voice:** Compare your company's media coverage in relation to competitors. For instance, if your company's share of voice in analyst reports has risen from 10% to 15%, it suggests an increased presence and influence.

- ✔ **Influence on Sales**: Analyze the impact of analyst recommendations or mentions on your sales figures. Suppose 20% of your B2B software sales are directly influenced by analyst endorsements. In that case, this data demonstrates the concrete impact of your AR program.

- ✔ **Customer Feedback:** Collect feedback from customers who have engaged with your company through AR programs. For example, if you receive glowing testimonials from customers who were positively influenced by analyst interactions, it reflects the value of AR efforts in building trust and relationships.

- ✔ **Market Perception:** Conduct surveys or assessments to gauge shifts in market perception and brand reputation influenced by AR activities. For instance, if a survey reveals that 70% of respondents perceive your company as a market leader due to analyst recommendations, it indicates success.

- ✔ **Analyst Briefings and Inquiries:** Measure the number and quality of analyst briefings and inquiries that your AR team conducts. If your team has conducted 100 high-quality briefings in a quarter, it signifies strong engagement and influence.

- ✔ **Competitive Analysis:** Assess how well your AR program positions your company in comparison to competitors in analyst reports and evaluations. If your company consistently ranks higher than competitors in Gartner Magic Quadrants, it demonstrates the program's effectiveness.

- ✔ **Lead Generation:** Track leads generated from analyst interactions and events. If the number of high-quality leads has increased by 40% due to AR activities, it signifies a successful program.

- ✔ **Market Share:** Monitor changes in your company's market share in relation to competitors. If your market share has grown by 5% over a year, and AR played a significant role, it reflects the program's impact.

- ✔ **Customer Retention**: Examine customer retention rates and loyalty among those influenced by AR interactions. For example, if customers engaged through AR have a 90% retention rate, it demonstrates the positive impact on customer relationships.

- ✔ **Media and Press Mentions:** Analyze media and press coverage related to your company that stems from AR activities. If your AR efforts have led to a 25% increase in positive media mentions, it illustrates the program's success.

- ✔ **Cost per Analyst Engagement:** Calculate the cost of running the AR program compared to the number and quality of analyst engagements. For example, if the cost per analyst engagement has decreased by 15%, it signifies cost-efficiency.

- ✔ **Analyst Satisfaction**: Gather feedback from analysts on their satisfaction with your AR program. Positive feedback can indicate successful collaboration. For instance, if 90% of analysts report satisfaction with your briefing process, it showcases effective engagement.

- ✔ **Web and Social Media Metrics**: Monitor web traffic and social media engagement resulting from analyst mentions and recommendations. If web traffic from social media has increased by 50% due to analyst-driven content, it reflects a positive outcome.

- ✔ **Thought Leadership:** Track the development of thought leadership content generated through AR, such as whitepapers, reports, and webinars. If the number of thought leadership pieces produced has doubled over a year, it indicates a growing influence in the industry.

Regularly tracking these metrics and KPIs can help AR professionals assess the success and impact of their efforts over the long term. However, to effectively maximize the Return on Investment (ROI) in Analyst Relations (AR), it's imperative to employ a strategic approach that encompasses various key elements. These elements not only enhance your engagement with industry analysts but also drive tangible business outcomes. By setting clear objectives and Key Performance Indicators (KPIs), efficiently allocating resources, and engaging in targeted relationship building, your AR program lays the foundation for success.

Moreover, strategic content creation and distribution, leveraging analyst insights for informed decision-making, continuous evaluation, and collaboration with internal stakeholders form the pillars of a robust AR strategy. Let's delve into these essential components, each contributing to the achievement of a strong ROI on your analyst relations investments

- **Setting Clear Objectives and Key Performance Indicators (KPIs):** Establishing clear objectives is fundamental to maximizing ROI in AR. Goals should be specific, measurable, achievable, relevant, and time-bound (SMART). Examples include enhancing positive analyst coverage, improving analyst ratings, and driving analyst recommendations. Aligning objectives with business goals allows for effective measurement and evaluation of ROI.

- **Efficient Resource Allocation:** Efficient allocation of resources plays a vital role in maximizing ROI. This involves optimizing budget, personnel, and time allocation to achieve desired outcomes. Prioritizing influential and relevant analysts ensures resources are allocated strategically, focusing efforts on those who have the greatest impact on the target audience.

- **Targeted Engagement and Relationship Building:** Targeted engagement and relationship building are essential for maximizing ROI in AR. Identifying influential analysts allows companies to build strong relationships with key individuals. Tailoring engagement strategies to address analysts' specific needs and preferences enhances the effectiveness of interactions, fostering valuable connections.

- ✔ **Strategic Content Creation and Distribution:** Strategic content creation and distribution contribute to maximizing ROI in AR. By creating high-quality and relevant content, companies position themselves as industry thought leaders. Distributing content through analyst briefings, reports, whitepapers, and webinars ensures that analysts have access to valuable insights, enhancing their perception of the company.

- ✔ **Leveraging Analyst Insights for Business Decisions**: Maximizing ROI in AR involves leveraging analyst insights to inform business decisions. Actively seeking analyst opinions, market research reports, and industry trends provides valuable insights. Integrating these insights into business strategies, product development, and go-to-market plans ensures AR efforts have a tangible impact on overall success.

- ✔ **Continuous Evaluation and Measurement:** Continuous evaluation and measurement are crucial for maximizing ROI in AR. Regularly assessing the effectiveness and impact of AR initiatives allows for data-driven adjustments. Tracking metrics such as analyst coverage, ratings, recommendations, and the influence of analyst insights on business decisions provides valuable feedback for improvement.

- ✔ **Collaboration with Internal Stakeholders**: Collaboration with internal stakeholders is essential in maximizing ROI in AR. Engaging with executives, product teams, sales, and marketing aligns AR strategies with broader business objectives. Leveraging analyst insights and endorsements to support sales efforts, enhance product positioning, and drive business growth strengthens the overall impact of AR.

By implementing these strategies and continually evaluating outcomes, companies can maximize the ROI of their AR efforts. This not only strengthens relationships with analysts but also drives positive business outcomes, ultimately achieving a strong ROI on their analyst relations investments.

Notes

Chapter **16**

THE ROLE OF ANALYST RELATIONS IN MERGERS AND ACQUISITIONS

Mergers and acquisitions (M&A) are complex business transactions that have a significant impact on companies and their stakeholders. In this chapter, we explore the crucial role of analyst relations (AR) in navigating the challenges and maximizing the benefits during M&A activities. By effectively managing communication, building relationships, and leveraging analyst insights, companies can enhance their M&A strategies and outcomes.

- **Strategic Communication Planning**: Effective communication is key to managing M&A activities and addressing concerns of analysts, investors, and other stakeholders. AR professionals play a crucial role in developing a strategic communication plan that ensures transparency, consistency, and clarity throughout the M&A process. This involves identifying key messages, target audiences, and appropriate communication channels to disseminate information in a timely and accurate manner.

- **Relationship Building with Analysts**: AR professionals should proactively engage with analysts during M&A activities to foster understanding and maintain trust. By establishing strong relationships with analysts, companies can navigate uncertainties and address potential misconceptions. Regular briefings, meetings, and updates keep analysts informed and provide an opportunity to address their concerns and gather valuable insights.

- ✓ **Analyst Perception and Influence:** Understanding analyst perceptions and influence is vital during M&A activities. AR professionals should monitor analyst reports, opinions, and industry commentary related to the transaction. By assessing analyst sentiment and identifying potential areas of concern or opportunity, companies can tailor their communications and engagement strategies to manage and shape analyst perception.

- ✓ **Leveraging Analyst Insights:** AR professionals can leverage analyst insights to inform M&A strategies and decision-making. Analysts possess in-depth knowledge of the industry landscape, competitive dynamics, and market trends. Engaging with analysts provides companies with valuable market intelligence, competitor analysis, and recommendations that can inform integration plans and post-merger positioning strategies.

- ✓ **Integration Planning and Execution:** During M&A activities, AR professionals contribute to integration planning and execution. This includes identifying synergies, defining joint messaging, and aligning analyst engagement strategies. By collaborating with internal stakeholders, AR professionals ensure a cohesive approach that supports the company's strategic goals, maintains analyst relationships, and mitigates potential disruptions or misunderstandings.

- ✓ **Managing Analyst Coverage and Expectations:** AR professionals play a crucial role in managing analyst coverage and expectations during M&A activities. By providing accurate and timely updates, companies can keep analysts informed about the progress and impact of the transaction. This helps maintain trust, reduces speculation, and aligns analyst coverage with the company's messaging and goals.

- ✓ **Post-Merger Analyst Relations:** AR efforts continue post-merger to ensure a smooth transition and ongoing positive relationships with analysts. AR professionals should facilitate integration-related briefings, product roadmaps, and executive meetings to address analysts' ongoing inquiries and provide updates on integration progress. This ongoing engagement helps sustain positive analyst sentiment and supports long-term business objectives.

- ✔ **Measurement and Evaluation:** Measuring the effectiveness of AR in M&A activities is crucial for assessing the impact and value of the efforts. Companies can evaluate the success of AR initiatives by tracking analyst coverage, sentiment, and recommendations related to the transaction. Additionally, feedback from analysts and internal stakeholders provides insights into the effectiveness of communication strategies and the perceived value of AR efforts during the M&A process.

In conclusion, analyst relations play a vital role in supporting successful M&A activities. AR professionals contribute by developing strategic communication plans, building relationships with analysts, leveraging their insights, supporting integration efforts, managing analyst coverage and expectations, and evaluating the effectiveness of AR initiatives. By effectively engaging with analysts throughout the M&A process, companies can enhance transparency, manage perceptions, and drive positive outcomes for all stakeholders involved.

Notes

CHAPTER 17

INFLUENCING INDUSTRY ANALYSTS' RESEARCH AGENDA

In the ever-evolving business landscape, industry analysts play a crucial role in shaping market perceptions and influencing decision-making. This chapter explores the significance of influencing industry analysts' research agenda aka his research calendar and provides insights into strategies that companies can employ to effectively shape analysts' focus and priorities. By understanding analysts' research processes, building relationships, and providing valuable insights, companies can exert influence and maximize the impact of analyst research.

- **Understanding the Analyst Research Process:** To effectively influence industry analysts' research agenda, it is essential to understand their research process. This involves gaining insights into how analysts identify research topics, conduct analysis, and produce reports. By understanding their methodologies, timelines, and areas of expertise, companies can tailor their approach to align with analysts' requirements and preferences.

- **Building Relationships with Industry Analysts:** Building strong relationships with industry analysts is crucial for influencing their research agenda. Establishing trust, credibility, and open lines of communication contribute to fostering meaningful relationships. Engaging with analysts through regular briefings, meetings, and events helps companies stay top of mind and ensures that analysts value their input and insights.

✔ **Providing Valuable Insights and Market Intelligence:** To influence analysts' research agenda, companies must provide valuable insights and market intelligence. Sharing unique perspectives, proprietary data, and industry trends contributes to shaping analysts' understanding of the market landscape. By providing analysts with timely and relevant information, companies position themselves as industry thought leaders and increase the likelihood of influencing their research direction.

✔ **Collaborating on Research Initiatives:** Collaboration with industry analysts on research initiatives can significantly influence their research agenda. By proactively suggesting research topics, participating in surveys, or offering access to subject matter experts, companies can drive analysts' interest in specific areas. Collaboration demonstrates a willingness to contribute to the research process and enhances the likelihood of influencing analysts' focus.

✔ **Engaging in Analyst Inquiries and Briefings:** Responding promptly and effectively to analyst inquiries and briefings is critical for influencing their research agenda. By providing comprehensive and insightful responses to inquiries, companies can shape analysts' understanding and influence the direction of their research. Proactively offering briefings on key initiatives, products, or market trends ensures that analysts are well-informed and more likely to consider these topics in their research.

✔ **Influencing Through Thought Leadership:** Establishing thought leadership in the industry is a powerful way to influence analysts' research agenda. By consistently publishing high-quality content, such as whitepapers, articles, and blog posts, companies can shape industry discourse and drive analysts' attention to specific topics. Demonstrating expertise, innovative thinking, and a deep understanding of market trends increases the likelihood of influencing analysts' research priorities.

✔ **Leveraging Analyst Relations Programs:** Effective management of analyst relations programs can significantly influence industry analysts' research agenda. By strategically leveraging resources, engaging in proactive outreach, and aligning messaging and activities with analysts' interests, companies can shape analysts' perception of their brand and steer their research focus toward areas that align with the company's strategic objectives.

- ✔ **Continuous Engagement and Relationship Nurturing:** Influencing industry analysts' research agenda requires ongoing engagement and relationship nurturing. Regular interactions, such as briefings, meetings, and events, help companies stay connected with analysts and maintain a position of influence. By continuously providing valuable insights, responding to inquiries, and nurturing relationships, companies can exert long-term influence on analysts' research agenda.

In conclusion, influencing industry analysts' research agenda requires a strategic approach that combines understanding their research process, building strong relationships, providing valuable insights, collaborating on research initiatives, engaging in analyst inquiries, establishing thought leadership, leveraging analyst relations programs, and nurturing continuous engagement. By effectively influencing analysts' research priorities, companies can shape market perceptions, drive industry discourse, and maximize the impact of analyst research on their business and the industry as a whole.

Notes

CHAPTER **18**

PARTNERING WITH SALES AND MARKETING FOR ANALYST RELATIONS SUCCESS

In today's competitive business landscape, effective collaboration between analyst relations (AR), sales, and marketing teams is essential for maximizing the impact and success of analyst relations initiatives. This chapter explores the significance of partnering with sales and marketing for analyst relations success and provides insights into strategies that foster alignment, enhance messaging, and drive positive outcomes. By working together, companies can leverage the power of combined efforts to influence analysts, drive sales enablement, and amplify brand presence.

- **Aligning Goals and Objectives:** Aligning the goals and objectives of AR, sales, and marketing teams is the first step toward successful collaboration. By fostering a shared vision and understanding of each team's priorities, companies can ensure that efforts are coordinated and focused on achieving common goals. This alignment sets the foundation for effective partnership and maximizes the impact of collective efforts.

- **Sharing Market Intelligence and Insights**: Sales and marketing teams possess valuable market intelligence and customer insights that can significantly enhance AR initiatives. By collaborating with these teams, AR professionals gain access to real-time feedback, customer pain points, and competitive analysis. This information enables them to tailor analyst engagements, messaging, and content to address market needs and maximize the relevance and impact of their interactions.

- ✔ **Coordinating Messaging and Positioning:** Consistent and coordinated messaging is critical for successful analyst relations. By partnering with sales and marketing, AR professionals can align their messaging with broader marketing and sales enablement efforts. This ensures that the company presents a cohesive and compelling narrative to analysts, enabling them to deliver consistent messages during analyst interactions and ultimately influencing analyst perceptions positively.

- ✔ **Sales Enablement through Analyst Insights:** AR teams can play a vital role in sales enablement by providing sales teams with analyst insights, research reports, and relevant industry analysis. This equips the sales force with valuable ammunition to address customer inquiries, overcome objections, and reinforce the company's credibility and market positioning. Collaborating with sales teams allows AR professionals to understand specific sales challenges and tailor analyst insights to support the sales process effectively.

- ✔ **Joint Analyst Engagement Strategies:** Collaborative planning and execution of analyst engagements enhance the effectiveness and impact of these interactions. AR, sales, and marketing teams can jointly develop analyst engagement strategies, ensuring consistent messaging and leveraging the unique strengths of each team. By aligning efforts, coordinating analyst briefings, and involving sales representatives in key interactions, companies can foster stronger analyst relationships and drive positive outcomes.

- ✔ **Co-creating Content and Thought Leadership:** Collaboration between AR, sales, and marketing teams can result in the co-creation of content and thought leadership initiatives. By leveraging sales and marketing expertise and aligning them with AR insights, companies can develop compelling content that resonates with analysts and customers alike. This joint effort positions the company as a thought leader in the industry and strengthens its influence on analysts' perceptions.

- ✔ **Sharing Success Stories:** Sharing success stories and showcasing the impact of analyst relations collaboration is an effective way to reinforce the value of the partnership. By highlighting instances where joint efforts resulted in positive analyst coverage, increased sales, or enhanced brand reputation, companies inspire further collaboration and foster a culture of teamwork between AR, sales, and marketing teams.

- ✔ **Continuous Communication and Feedback Loop:** Maintaining open lines of communication and establishing a feedback loop between AR, sales, and marketing teams is crucial for ongoing collaboration. Regular meetings, shared platforms, and collaborative tools enable the exchange of ideas, updates, and insights. By fostering a culture of continuous communication and feedback, companies can adapt strategies, optimize efforts, and further enhance analyst relations' success.

In conclusion, partnering with sales and marketing is integral to analyst relations success. By aligning goals, sharing market intelligence, coordinating messaging, enabling sales teams, developing joint analyst engagement strategies, co-creating content, sharing success stories, and maintaining continuous communication, companies can leverage the collective power of these teams to influence analysts, drive sales, and amplify their brand presence in the market. Collaborative efforts between AR, sales, and marketing teams foster synergy, enhance messaging consistency, and maximize the impact of analyst relations initiatives on overall business success.

Notes

Chapter **19**

BEST PRACTICES FOR ANALYST BRIEFINGS AND PRESENTATIONS

Analyst briefings and presentations are crucial components of successful analyst relations (AR) programs. These interactions provide opportunities to engage with industry analysts, share insights, and shape their perceptions of the company. This chapter explores best practices for conducting effective analyst briefings and presentations, enabling companies to deliver impactful and engaging sessions that drive positive analyst coverage and support business objectives.

- **Understand Analyst Needs and Objectives:** Before conducting an analyst briefing or presentation, it is essential to understand the specific needs, objectives, and areas of interest for the targeted analysts. Research their previous reports, coverage areas, and industry focus to tailor the content and messaging accordingly. This understanding helps create a more relevant and engaging session that addresses the analysts' specific concerns and adds value to their research.

- **Prepare a Clear and Concise Agenda:** Develop a clear and concise agenda for the analyst briefing or presentation. The agenda should outline the topics to be covered, the order of discussion, and allocated time for each section. This helps maintain a focused and organized session, ensuring that key points are addressed and enabling analysts to follow the flow of the presentation.

- ✔ **Craft Compelling and Relevant Content:** Create compelling and relevant content that aligns with the analysts' interests and research focus. Presentations should highlight the company's strategic initiatives, industry trends, competitive differentiators, and market insights. Use visuals, case studies, and data to support key messages and provide a comprehensive understanding of the company's value proposition.

- ✔ **Engage in Two-Way Dialogue:** Encourage an open and interactive discussion during analyst briefings and presentations. Allow time for questions and encourage analysts to share their perspectives and insights. This two-way dialogue fosters engagement, demonstrates a willingness to listen, and provides an opportunity to address any concerns or misconceptions raised by the analysts.

- ✔ **Showcase Customer Success Stories:** Incorporate customer success stories and testimonials into the analyst briefing or presentation. Highlighting real-world examples of how the company's solutions or services have delivered tangible value to customers adds credibility and demonstrates the practical application of the company's offerings. Analysts appreciate the opportunity to hear about concrete results and the impact on customers' businesses.

- ✔ **Provide Differentiation and Competitive Analysis:** Highlight the company's differentiation and competitive advantages during the analyst briefing or presentation. Clearly articulate how the company stands out from competitors, what sets its solutions apart, and how it addresses market challenges. Providing a comprehensive competitive analysis enables analysts to evaluate the company's position in the market and strengthens their confidence in its capabilities.

- ✔ **Support Claims with Data and Research:** Back up key claims and statements with relevant data, market research, and industry reports. Analysts rely on data-driven insights to inform their research and recommendations. Providing credible and substantiated information enhances the company's credibility and positions it as a trusted source of industry intelligence.

- ✔ **Tailor Presentations to Different Analyst Roles:** Consider the diverse roles and interests of the analysts participating in the briefing or presentation. Tailor the content and messaging to address the specific needs of different analyst roles, such as technology-focused analysts, industry-specific analysts, or market trend analysts. This customization ensures that each analyst receives information relevant to their areas of expertise and helps maximize the impact of the session.

- ✔ **Follow-Up and Provide Additional Resources:** After the briefing or presentation, follow up with the analysts to address any outstanding questions or requests for further information. Provide additional resources such as whitepapers, research reports, or access to subject matter experts to support their ongoing research. This post-session engagement reinforces the company's commitment to analyst relations and contributes to long-term positive relationships.

- ✔ **Continuously Seek Feedback and Improve:** Seek feedback from analysts to understand their perspectives on the briefing or presentation. Evaluate the effectiveness of the session and identify areas for improvement. Use the feedback to refine future briefings and presentations, ensuring continuous enhancement of the company's analyst engagement efforts.

By following these best practices, companies can conduct effective and impactful analyst briefings and presentations. These interactions provide opportunities to shape analysts' perceptions, drive positive coverage, and support business objectives. By delivering tailored content, engaging in two-way dialogue, showcasing customer success stories, providing competitive analysis, and continuously seeking feedback, companies can foster strong relationships with industry analysts and maximize the value of their analyst relations efforts.

Notes

CHAPTER **20**

MANAGING ANALYST RELATIONS IN A GLOBAL CONTEXT

In today's interconnected world, managing analyst relations (AR) in a global context presents unique challenges and opportunities. The relationship between industry analysts and companies can take various forms, depending on the nature of the interaction and the objectives of both parties. Here are some different types of relations between analysts and companies:

- **Advisory Relationships:** Analysts often have advisory roles, where they provide strategic guidance to companies. Companies may have ongoing advisory contracts with specific analysts or analyst firms to gain insights and recommendations.

- **Vendor Briefings:** Companies engage with analysts to provide them with in-depth information about their products, services, and strategies. These briefings help analysts stay updated and enable companies to influence analyst perceptions.

- **Market Research:** Companies may commission analyst firms to conduct specific market research or custom reports to gather insights about their industry, competition, and market trends.

- ✓ **Vendor-Sponsored Research:** In some cases, companies sponsor research projects conducted by analysts, with the aim of influencing the research outcomes in their favor.

- ✓ **Briefings and Inquiries:** Companies often hold regular briefings and inquiries with analysts to keep them informed about their latest developments, answer questions, and gain feedback.

- ✓ **Events and Conferences:** Companies may invite analysts to their events, conferences, or user group meetings, allowing them to witness their products and services firsthand and fostering relationships.

- ✓ **Analyst Relations Programs:** Companies may have dedicated AR programs with teams responsible for building and managing relationships with analysts, ensuring they have access to relevant information and expert spokespeople.

- ✓ **Customized Engagements:** Companies tailor their engagements with analysts based on their specific needs and the analysts' interests. This can involve custom research, workshops, or deep-dive sessions.

- ✓ **Content Creation:** Companies create thought leadership content such as whitepapers, webinars, and reports to share with analysts, positioning themselves as industry leaders.

- ✓ **Competitive Analysis:** Analysts often conduct competitive analysis and benchmarking. Companies may engage with analysts to ensure they are favorably positioned in comparison to competitors.

- ✓ **Sales Support:** Companies leverage analyst insights and endorsements to support their sales efforts, such as sharing analyst reports and recommendations with potential customers.

- ✓ **Product Briefings:** Companies provide analysts with detailed information about new product launches and updates to gain their perspectives and recommendations.

- ✓ **Influencer Relations:** Beyond traditional industry analysts, companies may engage with broader influencer communities, including bloggers, vloggers, and industry experts.

- ✓ **Custom Events:** Companies organize events or roundtable discussions with analysts to delve into specific topics or challenges that are of mutual interest.

- ✓ **Feedback and Insights Gathering:** Companies may actively seek analyst opinions, market research reports, and industry trends to inform their business strategies, product development, and marketing plans.

- ✓ **Collaboration on Marketing Campaigns:** Some companies collaborate with analysts on joint marketing campaigns, such as webinars or co-authored content. The specific type of relationship can vary based on the company's goals, industry, and the focus of the analysts. Building and nurturing these relationships is an important aspect of an effective Analyst Relations program and can significantly impact a company's market perception and business success.

This chapter explores the importance of effectively navigating cultural differences, regional nuances, and diverse analyst landscapes in global AR programs. By understanding global dynamics, adapting strategies, and building strong relationships, companies can successfully manage analyst relations across different regions and maximize the impact of their AR efforts.

- ✓ **Recognize Cultural Differences and Regional Nuances:** Cultural differences and regional nuances significantly influence analyst relations in a global context. Understanding and respecting these variations is essential for successful engagement. AR professionals should familiarize themselves with cultural norms, communication styles, and business practices in different regions. This awareness enables the adaptation of strategies and approaches to better resonate with analysts in each specific cultural context.

- ✔ **Tailor Messaging and Content to Local Markets:** One-size-fits-all messaging may not effectively resonate with analysts in diverse global markets. To maximize the impact of AR efforts, tailor messaging and content to address specific local market needs and preferences. Consider factors such as language, market maturity, regulatory requirements, and industry trends when crafting messages and delivering presentations. This localized approach demonstrates a commitment to understanding and addressing regional dynamics.

- ✔ **Leverage Local Analyst Relationships and Expertise:** Building strong relationships with local analysts is critical for success in global AR programs. Engage with local analysts who possess deep knowledge of the regional market and industry landscape. Leverage their expertise to gain insights into local trends, customer preferences, and competitive dynamics. Collaborating with local analysts also strengthens the company's credibility and understanding of regional nuances.

- ✔ **Understand Local Analyst Firms and Influencers:** Each region has its own unique landscape of analyst firms and influential analysts. Research and identify the key local analyst firms and influential individuals relevant to the company's industry. Understand their areas of expertise, coverage focus, and client base. Tailor engagement strategies to effectively reach and engage with these local analyst firms and influencers to maximize the impact of AR efforts in the specific region.

- ✔ **Establish Consistent Global Messaging:** While tailoring messaging to local markets is important, maintaining consistent global messaging is equally crucial. Develop a core set of messaging and positioning that aligns with the company's overall strategic goals and value proposition. This ensures a unified message across different regions while allowing for appropriate customization based on local market dynamics.

- ✔ **Coordinate Global and Regional AR Efforts:** Effective coordination between global and regional AR teams is essential for managing analyst relations in a global context. Establish clear lines of communication, collaboration, and information sharing between global and regional teams.

This coordination ensures consistency in messaging, aligns goals and objectives, and avoids duplication of efforts. Regular global and regional AR team meetings facilitate strategic alignment and knowledge exchange.

✔ **Facilitate Knowledge Sharing and Best Practices**: Encourage knowledge sharing and best practice sharing among global and regional AR teams. Create platforms, such as regular meetings, virtual collaboration spaces, and knowledge repositories, to facilitate the exchange of insights, experiences, and successful strategies. This collective learning enables teams to leverage each other's expertise and adapt effective practices to different regions.

✔ **Embrace Virtual Engagement and Communication**: In a global context, virtual engagement and communication play a vital role in managing analyst relations. Leverage technology and virtual platforms to conduct analyst briefings, meetings, and presentations. Virtual engagement enables efficient and cost-effective interactions with analysts across different time zones and geographic locations. Embrace virtual tools to maintain regular communication and build relationships with analysts globally.

✔ **Stay Abreast of Regional Market Dynamics and Trends**: Continuously monitor regional market dynamics, industry trends, and regulatory changes in different regions. This knowledge helps AR professionals adapt strategies and messaging to remain relevant and responsive to local market conditions. Staying abreast of regional developments also positions the company as a trusted source of industry intelligence and strengthens relationships with analysts.

✔ **Foster Cultural Sensitivity and Adaptability**: In managing analyst relations in a global context, cultural sensitivity and adaptability are crucial. Embrace diverse perspectives, respect cultural differences, and demonstrate adaptability to local business customs and practices. Building relationships based on trust, mutual respect, and a genuine understanding of local cultures enhances the effectiveness of AR efforts in a global context.

By recognizing cultural differences, tailoring messaging to local markets, leveraging local relationships, understanding local analyst firms, establishing consistent global messaging, coordinating global and regional efforts, facilitating knowledge sharing, embracing virtual engagement, staying informed about regional dynamics, and fostering cultural sensitivity, companies can effectively manage analyst relations in a global context. Successful global AR programs build strong relationships, drive positive coverage, and support business objectives across diverse markets and regions.

CHAPTER 21

ADDRESSING CHALLENGES AND PITFALLS IN ANALYST RELATIONS

While analyst relations (AR) programs can yield significant benefits, they also come with their share of challenges and potential pitfalls. This chapter explores common challenges faced in analyst relations and provides strategies for effectively addressing them. By proactively addressing these challenges, companies can strengthen their analyst relationships, navigate potential pitfalls, and maximize the impact of their AR efforts.

- **Managing Analyst Expectations**: Analysts often have high expectations and varying demands. It is important to manage these expectations effectively. Clearly communicate the company's capabilities, product roadmap, and strategic direction, while also setting realistic expectations regarding what can be shared and when. Establish open lines of communication to address any misconceptions or unmet expectations promptly, fostering transparency and trust.

- **Dealing with Negative Analyst Coverage:** Negative analyst coverage can be challenging, but it is important to approach it constructively. Instead of avoiding or ignoring negative coverage, engage in open dialogue with analysts to understand their concerns and address any misperceptions. Providing evidence-based counterarguments, sharing customer success stories, and seeking opportunities for improvement can help turn negative coverage into positive outcomes.

- ✓ **Overcoming Budget Constraints:** Limited budget allocation for analyst relations can pose challenges. To overcome this, focus on strategic prioritization and resource optimization. Identify key analysts who have the most influence in the company's target market and allocate resources accordingly. Leverage cost-effective alternatives such as virtual engagements, regional roundtable discussions, and social media platforms to maximize the impact of AR efforts within budget constraints.

- ✓ **Balancing Analyst Engagement:** Engaging with a diverse group of analysts across different firms and regions can be demanding. It is crucial to strike a balance and prioritize engagements based on their strategic value. Segment analysts based on their influence, alignment with business objectives, and relevance to target markets. Tailor engagement strategies to focus on the key analysts who have the greatest impact on the company's success.

- ✓ **Aligning AR with Shifting Market Dynamics:** The business landscape is constantly evolving, and market dynamics change rapidly. AR programs must adapt to these shifts to remain effective. Continuously monitor market trends, competitive landscapes, and emerging technologies to ensure that AR strategies align with changing market dynamics. Regularly review and update messaging, positioning, and engagement strategies to stay relevant and responsive to market changes.

- ✓ **Overcoming Organizational Silos:** AR programs often encounter challenges related to organizational silos and lack of cross-functional collaboration. To address this, foster collaboration and communication with internal stakeholders such as marketing, sales, product management, and executive leadership. Educate and align internal teams on the value of AR, establish shared goals, and encourage cross-functional collaboration to maximize the impact of AR efforts.

- ✓ **Building Long-Term Relationships:** Building and nurturing long-term relationships with analysts require sustained effort and consistent engagement. Avoid treating analyst relations as a one-time or ad hoc activity. Invest in building strong relationships based on mutual trust and ongoing dialogue. Regularly update analysts on the company's progress, involve them in key initiatives, and seek their input to maintain long-term relationships that drive sustained positive coverage and influence.

✔ **Evaluating and Demonstrating ROI:** Measuring and demonstrating the return on investment (ROI) of AR programs can be challenging. Define key performance indicators (KPIs) aligned with business objectives and track metrics such as analyst coverage, influence, and impact on sales and market perception. Collect feedback from internal stakeholders and analysts to evaluate the effectiveness of AR efforts. Leverage data and analytics to showcase the tangible value of AR in supporting business goals.

✔ **Anticipating and Addressing Analyst Turnover:** Analyst turnover is a common challenge in AR, as analysts may change roles, switch firms, or leave the industry. To mitigate the impact of analyst turnover, maintain relationships beyond individual analysts. Engage with analyst firms, understand their succession plans, and proactively build relationships with new analysts who join or replace departing ones. Continuity in engagement and knowledge sharing helps navigate analyst transitions smoothly.

✔ **Staying Ethical and Transparent:** Maintaining ethical standards and transparency is vital in analyst relations. Avoid engaging in unethical practices, such as offering financial incentives for positive coverage or suppressing negative analyst opinions. Foster an environment of transparency, integrity, and open communication. Compliance with industry regulations and guidelines ensures a trusted and ethical approach to analyst relations.

By proactively addressing these challenges and pitfalls in analyst relations, companies can strengthen their AR programs, build stronger relationships with analysts, and maximize the impact of their efforts. Effective management of analyst expectations, addressing negative coverage, optimizing resources, balancing engagement, adapting to market dynamics, fostering collaboration, building long-term relationships, measuring ROI, addressing analyst turnover, and maintaining ethical practices contribute to successful analyst relations programs.

Notes

CHAPTER 22

ENHANCING ANALYST RELATIONS THROUGH THOUGHT LEADERSHIP

Thought leadership plays a crucial role in strengthening analyst relations (AR) and positioning a company as a trusted industry expert. This chapter explores the significance of thought leadership in analyst relations and provides strategies for enhancing AR through thought leadership initiatives. By demonstrating expertise, driving industry conversations, and providing valuable insights, companies can build stronger analyst relationships and elevate their standing in the market.

- **Establishing a Clear Thought Leadership Strategy:** Develop a clear thought leadership strategy that aligns with the company's business objectives and target audience. Identify the key topics, industry trends, and areas of expertise that are relevant to analysts and their research focus. Craft a thought leadership plan that outlines the goals, target audience, content formats, and distribution channels to effectively engage with analysts and establish the company as a thought leader.

- **Identifying Industry Trends and Insights:** Stay abreast of industry trends, emerging technologies, and market dynamics. Conduct in-depth research, gather market intelligence, and monitor industry reports and analyst insights. By identifying and analyzing industry trends, companies can provide valuable insights to analysts, positioning themselves as reliable sources of market intelligence and driving conversations around key industry topics.

- ✔ **Developing High-Quality Content:** Create high-quality content that showcases the company's expertise, research, and unique perspectives. Develop whitepapers, research reports, case studies, and blog articles that offer thought-provoking analysis, actionable insights, and innovative ideas. Content should be well-researched, data-driven, and supported by credible sources to enhance its credibility and value to analysts.

- ✔ **Engaging in Industry Events and Conferences:** Participate actively in industry events, conferences, and webinars to share thought leadership with analysts and industry influencers. Deliver keynote speeches, participate in panel discussions, and host webinars on relevant topics. These engagements provide opportunities to present the company's insights, engage in meaningful discussions, and foster relationships with analysts who attend these events.

- ✔ **Collaborating with Analysts on Research Projects:** Collaborate with analysts on research projects to enhance thought leadership and strengthen analyst relationships. Explore opportunities to co-author reports, contribute insights, or participate in surveys and research studies conducted by analyst firms. This collaboration demonstrates a commitment to industry thought leadership and helps shape the research agenda, positioning the company as a trusted partner to analysts.

- ✔ **Leveraging Digital Channels and Social Media:** Harness the power of digital channels and social media platforms to amplify thought leadership efforts. Share content, research findings, and industry insights through the company's website, blog, social media accounts, and industry-specific forums. Engage in conversations, respond to analyst inquiries, and actively participate in online discussions to establish a strong digital presence and expand reach to analysts.

- **Encouraging Executive Thought Leadership:** Foster executive thought leadership by encouraging company leaders to actively engage with analysts. Encourage executives to participate in analyst briefings, provide insights, and contribute to thought leadership content. Executive involvement enhances the company's credibility, demonstrates leadership expertise, and deepens analyst relationships.

- **Tailoring Thought Leadership for Different Analyst Audiences:** Understand the different audiences within the analyst community and tailor thought leadership initiatives to meet their specific needs. Technology-focused analysts may require in-depth technical insights, while industry-specific analysts may be more interested in vertical-specific trends and case studies. Customize thought leadership content and messaging to resonate with the diverse analyst audience, maximizing its relevance and impact.

- **Measuring the Impact of Thought Leadership:** Establish metrics to measure the impact of thought leadership initiatives on analyst relations. Track key performance indicators (KPIs) such as increased analyst coverage, positive analyst opinions, inclusion in analyst reports, and analyst recommendations. Collect feedback from analysts on the value and usefulness of thought leadership content. Analyze website traffic, social media engagement, and content downloads to gauge the reach and resonance of thought leadership efforts.

- **Continuously Evolving Thought Leadership Strategy:** Thought leadership is an ongoing endeavor that requires continuous evolution. Monitor industry trends, feedback from analysts, and the evolving needs of the analyst community. Regularly assess and refine the thought leadership strategy to align with changing market dynamics, industry shifts, and emerging topics of interest. Stay agile and adapt thought leadership efforts to maintain relevance and effectiveness in AR programs.

By enhancing analyst relations through thought leadership, companies can establish themselves as trusted industry experts and thought leaders. By developing a clear thought leadership strategy, identifying industry trends and insights, creating high-quality content, engaging in industry events, collaborating with analysts, leveraging digital channels, encouraging executive thought leadership, tailoring content for different analyst audiences, measuring impact, and continuously evolving the thought leadership strategy, companies can strengthen their analyst relationships, drive positive coverage, and position themselves as leaders in their respective industries.

CHAPTER **23**

THE FUTURE OF ANALYST RELATIONS

As technology continues to evolve at an unprecedented rate, so too must the practice of analyst relations. In order to remain relevant and effective, AR professionals must adapt to the changing landscape of the industry and engage with influencers in new and innovative ways.

One of the most significant trends in the future of analyst relations is the increasing importance of social media and digital platforms. Analysts are no longer confined to traditional media outlets like print publications and broadcast news. Instead, they have a wide range of digital channels at their disposal, including blogs, podcasts, and social media platforms like Twitter and LinkedIn. This means that AR professionals must be adept at engaging with influencers across a variety of digital channels and must be able to tailor their messaging to suit each platform.

Another important trend in the future of analyst relations is the growing importance of data and analytics. As technology companies become more data-driven, analysts are increasingly expected to provide insights and recommendations based on data analysis. This means that AR professionals must be able to provide analysts with the data and insights they need to form informed opinions about a company or product. They must also be able to communicate these insights effectively to analysts and help them to understand the implications of the data for the company's strategy.

Finally, the future of analyst relations will be shaped by the continued growth of the influencer marketing industry. As more and more companies turn to influencers to help them reach new audiences and drive sales, AR professionals must be able to navigate the complex world of influencer marketing and build strong relationships with key influencers. This will require a deep understanding of the influencer landscape, as well as the ability to identify the right influencers for a particular company or product.

In summary, the future of analyst relations will be shaped by a range of trends, including the growing importance of digital platforms, the increasing importance of data and analytics, and the continued growth of the influencer marketing industry.

For Example, Artificial Intelligence (AI) has the potential to significantly impact analyst relations in various ways

Here are a few ways AI can change the landscape of analyst relations:

- **Automated Insights and Recommendations:** AI-powered analytics platforms can analyze vast amounts of data, identify patterns, and generate valuable insights and recommendations. Analysts can leverage these automated insights to augment their research and analysis, enabling them to provide more comprehensive and accurate assessments of companies, products, and market trends.

- **Personalized Research and Recommendations:** AI algorithms can personalize research and recommendations based on individual analyst preferences and interests. By understanding an analyst's focus areas, AI systems can deliver tailored insights, reports, and content that align with their specific needs, enabling more efficient and targeted engagements between analysts and technology companies.

- **Natural Language Processing and Sentiment Analysis:** AI-powered natural language processing (NLP) can process and analyze vast amounts of textual data, including news articles, social media posts, and analyst reports. This capability allows technology companies to monitor and assess sentiment, identify emerging trends, and track market perceptions in real-time, providing valuable inputs for analyst relations strategies.

- **Virtual Analyst Assistants**: AI-powered virtual assistants can provide analysts with on-demand access to relevant information, industry data, and research. These assistants can help analysts streamline their workflows, improve productivity, and stay updated on the latest developments, enabling them to deliver more informed insights and recommendations.

- **Augmented Influencer Identification:** AI algorithms can analyze social media profiles, online interactions, and content consumption patterns to identify and prioritize influential analysts and thought leaders. This capability helps technology companies focus their analyst relations efforts on the most relevant influencers and build stronger relationships with key industry voices.

- **Enhanced Predictive Analytics:** AI can enhance predictive analytics capabilities, enabling technology companies to anticipate market trends, customer behavior, and competitive dynamics. Analysts can leverage these predictive insights to provide forward-looking analysis and strategic recommendations to their clients, helping companies navigate the evolving technological landscape.

- AR professionals must be prepared to adapt to these trends and engage with influencers in new and innovative ways in order to build strong relationships and drive business results for their companies.

23.1 Some Industry Examples

In the ever-evolving tech landscape, numerous technology companies have recognized the importance of analyst relations in shaping market perceptions, enhancing brand visibility, and driving business growth. Let's explore a few real-world examples that illustrate the impact of effective analyst relations strategies:

Apple, renowned for its innovative products, has established a robust analyst relations team that engages with influential analysts from Gartner, a leading research and advisory firm. Through positive relationships, Apple ensures its products receive coverage in Gartner reports, gaining valuable market visibility and bolstering its reputation among customers and investors.

Similarly, Microsoft, a technology giant, maintains an extensive analyst relations program and collaborates closely with analysts from Forrester Research. By leveraging these relationships, Microsoft gains invaluable insights into market trends, competitive analysis, and feedback on its products and services. This feedback enables Microsoft to refine its strategies, enhance its offerings, and maintain a competitive edge in the tech industry.

Another notable example is Salesforce, a leading provider of customer relationship management (CRM) solutions. Salesforce understands the significance of analyst relations and actively engages with analysts from IDC (International Data Corporation). By leveraging IDC's market research and expert insights, Salesforce strengthens its market positioning, gains credibility, and builds trust among potential customers and investors.

Additionally, Amazon Web Services (AWS), the cloud computing division of Amazon, prioritizes building relationships with key industry influencers in the cloud computing space. By engaging with influential thought leaders, bloggers, and experts, AWS amplifies its brand awareness, educates customers about its services, and drives the adoption of cloud technologies.

These real-world examples underscore the strategic importance of analyst relations for technology companies. By proactively engaging with analysts and influencers, these companies enhance their market position, shape perceptions, and stay at the forefront of an ever-changing industry. From Apple to Microsoft, Salesforce to AWS, effective analyst relations play a pivotal role in driving success and maintaining a competitive edge in the dynamic tech landscape

23.2 My Final Thoughts

Managing analyst relations is a critical aspect of any technology company's success. In the ever-changing landscape of the tech industry, analysts play a crucial role in shaping the market's perception of your product or service. As a product marketing, analyst relations manager, PR manager, or influencer relationship manager, building stronger relationships with tech influencers is an essential part of your job.

Throughout this book, we have discussed various strategies and tips for building strong relationships with tech analysts. We have covered how to identify the right analysts for your company, how to approach them, how to keep them engaged, and how to leverage their insights to improve your product or service.

Remember that analysts are people too. They have their preferences, their biases, and their agendas. It's crucial to understand their motivations and to tailor your approach accordingly. The key to building a strong relationship with an analyst is to show them that you value their insights and expertise.

Another critical factor in managing analyst relations is transparency. Be open and honest with analysts about your product or service's strengths and weaknesses. Don't try to sugarcoat things or hide negative feedback. Instead, use their feedback as an opportunity to improve your product or service.

Finally, remember that managing analyst relations is an ongoing process. It's not a one-time event. You need to stay engaged with analysts regularly, provide them with updates on your product or service, and seek their feedback on an ongoing basis.

In conclusion, managing analyst relations is crucial for any technology company's success. By building strong relationships with tech influencers, you can shape the market's perception of your product or service and gain a competitive advantage. Remember to be transparent, show value, and stay engaged, and you'll be well on your way toward building strong relationships with tech analysts.

Notes

GLOSSARY OF ANALYST TERMS

In the world of technology companies, analysts play a significant role in shaping the opinions of potential customers, investors, and industry leaders. As a result, it is essential for product marketing, analyst relations managers, PR managers, and influencer relationship managers to understand the terminology used by analysts. This glossary aims to provide a comprehensive list of the most commonly used analyst terms.

- **Magic Quadrant**: A research methodology used by Gartner to analyze and evaluate technology vendors in a specific market. The quadrant is divided into four categories: Leaders, Challengers, Visionaries, and Niche Players.

- **Wave**: A research methodology used by Forrester to analyze and evaluate technology vendors in a specific market. The wave is divided into three categories: Leaders, Strong Performers, and Contenders.

- **SWOT Analysis:** A strategic planning tool used to evaluate the strengths, weaknesses, opportunities, and threats of a company, product, or service.

- **ROI: Return on Investment.** A measure of the profitability of an investment, typically expressed as a percentage.

- **TCO: Total Cost of Ownership.** A comprehensive assessment of all direct and indirect costs associated with a product or service.

- **Market Share:** The percentage of total sales in a specific market that a company or product holds.

- **Competitive Landscape:** The analysis of the competitive environment in a specific market, including the strengths and weaknesses of competitors, market trends, and potential threats.

- **Disruptive Technology:** A technology that fundamentally changes the way businesses operate or consumers live their lives.

- **Innovation:** The introduction of new ideas, methods, or products that create significant value for a company or its customers.

These are just a few of the many terms used by analysts in the technology industry. By understanding and utilizing these terms, product marketing, analyst relations managers, PR managers, and influencer relationship managers can build stronger relationships with analysts and better position their products or services in the market.

CAUTIONS

The following page serves as a general cautionary statement to readers of this book. It is important to acknowledge that the information contained within this book is provided for educational and informational purposes only. The content presented is based on general knowledge and understanding up to September 2021, and it may not reflect the most current updates or developments in the field of SaaS marketing. Readers are advised to conduct their own research and consult with professionals or experts for specific advice or guidance related to their individual circumstances.

No Legal or Professional Advice

The information presented in this book is not intended to serve as legal, financial, or professional advice. While efforts have been made to ensure the accuracy and reliability of the information provided, the author and publisher make no claims, promises, or guarantees about the completeness, accuracy, or suitability of the content.

Readers should not rely solely on the information presented in this book and should seek professional advice from qualified experts or consultants regarding their specific situations.

Use of Trademarks and Copyrighted Material

Throughout this book, certain trademarks, product names, company names, and copyrighted material may be mentioned. The inclusion of such material is for illustrative purposes only and does not imply endorsement, affiliation, or sponsorship by the respective owners. The author and publisher do not intend to infringe upon any intellectual property rights, and any use of trademarks or copyrighted material is done in accordance with fair use guidelines. Readers are advised to respect intellectual property rights and seek appropriate permissions or licenses when using third-party material.

Speculative Commentary and Future Predictions

In certain chapters or sections, the author may provide speculative commentary, predictions, or insights regarding SaaS marketing, industry trends, or emerging technologies. These speculations are based on the author's personal interpretation and assessment and should not be considered as factual or guaranteed. The future is inherently uncertain, and actual outcomes may differ from the author's predictions. Readers are encouraged to exercise their own judgment and conduct additional research before making any business decisions based on speculative commentary or predictions.

Limitation of Liability

The author and publisher of this book disclaim any liability for any loss, damage, or injury caused by the use or reliance upon the information presented herein. The content provided is on an "as-is" basis without warranties of any kind, express or implied. The author and publisher shall not be held responsible for any direct, indirect, incidental, consequential, or special damages arising out of or in connection with the use of this book.

Personal Responsibility

Readers are solely responsible for the interpretation and application of the information presented in this book. The author and publisher cannot be held liable for any decisions, actions, or outcomes resulting from the implementation of the ideas or strategies discussed. It is essential for readers to exercise their own discretion, perform due diligence, and seek professional advice when necessary to ensure the suitability and effectiveness of any strategies or recommendations provided.

In conclusion, this caution page serves as a reminder that the content presented in this book is intended for general information purposes only. Readers are encouraged to exercise their own judgment, conduct independent research, and seek professional advice before making any business or investment decisions. The author and publisher disclaim any responsibility for the accuracy, completeness, or applicability of the information contained within this book.